Resounding Pray

The Noon Bells and Hunyadi's Victory

by

Dr.ant

Resounding Pray: The Noon Bells and Hunyadi's Victory

Contents

Introduction

The annals of history, oft inscribed with tales of valor, unveil the grand narrative of a figure whose deeds echo through the corridors of time - John Hunyadi. The hero of our tale, whose name resounds like an ancient hymn, stood staunch as a bastion against the swelling tide of the Ottoman advance. His feats at the Battle of Belgrade merit immortalization, not solely for their strategic brilliance but also for the miraculous undertones that hallowed that day.

The mid-15th century, an epoch bristling with turmoil and transition, saw Christendom clasped in the throes of existential peril. The Ottoman Empire, driven by an insatiable ambition, cast its immense shadow across Europe, threatening to extinguish the vestiges of Christian dominion. In this dire crucible, the embers of Hunyadi's resolve ignited, manifesting in a series of military campaigns that would eventually culminate at the gates of Belgrade.

John Hunyadi, born to the lineage of knights and steeped in the fires of martial training, embodied the quintessence of chivalric duty. His early life, replete with trials, forged a spirit indomitable and a mind sharpened for the intricate art of warfare. He rose as a beacon of hope, a commander whose strategic acumen was matched only by his unshakeable faith.

As the Ottoman menace loomed large, the importance of a unified Christian front became paramount. The clarion call for such unity found a formidable ally in Pope Callixtus III, whose decrees resonated across the kingdoms of Europe. The papal edict for noon bells, summoning all to prayer, encapsulated the collective yearning for divine intercession against the potent threat. This unison of faith and arms gestured towards a sanctified struggle that transcended the mere physicality of battle.

The Battle of Belgrade, however, was not to be a mere collision of militaries but a theatre where fate and faith entwined. On the dusty plains and upon the ramparts, Hunyadi's forces, though outnumbered, displayed a synchronicity of movement and a fervor that belied their numbers. The meticulous preparations, alliances forged in the crucible of impending conflict, and revolutionary military reforms under Hunyadi's command painted a tableau of preparedness and providence poised for confrontation.

Yet, the chronicles recount more than martial prowess; they whisper of divine favor. Eyewitnesses recount moments of inexplicable occurrences, strokes of fortune that lent credence to the belief that celestial forces interceded on behalf of Hunyadi's legions. Whether it was the strategic inspiration that guided his maneuvers or the inexplicable shifts in battlefield dynamics, a pall of the miraculous shrouded the events in a tapestry of divine narrative.

As our account unfolds, it will dissect not only the tangible and tactical elements of this historic victory but will also delve into the theological implications that arose in its aftermath. The ripples of Belgrade were felt across the tapestry of Europe, reverberating through the church bells that rang out at noon, a practice that would strengthen the sinews of European unity and foster an enduring bond of faith.

The significance of Hunyadi's triumph resonates far beyond the confines of his era. In retrospect, we discern the broader canvas upon which these events played out, one that saw the emboldenment of Christian Europe, the safeguarding of its cultural and religious heritage, and the laying of seedbeds for the resurgence that would blossom into the Renaissance. It was not merely a battle won but a epochal pivot towards a fortified Christendom and an intertwined European destiny.

The legacy of John Hunyadi, etched in the hearts and minds of not only Hungarians but of all Christendom, serves as an enduring testament to the potency of faith and the resilience of a people besieged yet unyielding. His post-battle reforms and continued efforts ensured that the victories on the battlefield were translated into tangible fortifications of societal and political structures. His influence, thus, permeated beyond immediate conquests, embedding itself into the very fabric of European history.

As this narrative unfurls, it invites the reader to traverse the landscapes of historical upheaval, divine wonder, and the formidable will of a hero who stood as the guardian of Christendom in its darkest hours. The Battle of Belgrade, under Hunyadi's fierce leadership and underpinned by miraculous portents, marks a fulcrum around which the future course of Christian Europe pivoted. Thus, we embark upon this tale, a storied journey through an epoch where history's hues are painted with the deft strokes of courage, faith, and providence.

Chapter 1: The Siege of Constantinople

The grand city of Constantinople, resplendent with its towering walls and rich mosaics, found itself under siege that fateful year of 1453, a fulcrum upon which history would pivot. The Byzantine Empire, a beacon of art and knowledge, stood bravely against the relentless tide of the Ottoman forces. Cannons roared, and the city's mighty fortifications, once thought impregnable, trembled under the onslaught. Brave defenders mustered all their martial prowess and ingenuity, wielding both ancient stratagems and nascent technology in a desperate bid to stave off the doom encroaching upon their hallowed halls. Though the besieging force was vast and tenacious, the valor of Constantinople's defenders became the stuff of legend, setting a stage for an epochal confrontation destined to reverberate through the annals of time.

Cultural Background of Constantinople

To comprehend the Siege of Constantinople in its entirety, one must first delve into the rich and complex cultural tapestry of this renowned city, whose glory and grandeur once lit up the Byzantine Empire as the noonday sun. Constantinople, now known as Istanbul, stood as a bridge between East and West, a city that was both a fortress and a beacon of civilization, philosophy, and faith.

This illustrious metropolis carried the legacy of two empires—Roman and Byzantine. Its foundation, set by Constantine the Great in 330 AD, marked the city's rise as the new Rome. Adorned with magnificent edifices, grandiose cathedrals, and bustling markets, Constantinople was the heart of Eastern Orthodox Christianity. The city's great Hagia Sophia, with its awe-inspiring dome reaching toward the heavens, stood as a testament to the spiritual zeal and architectural genius of its people.

A land imbued with diverse cultural influences, Constantinople nurtured a society that valued education, artistry, and theological debate. The streets were teeming with scholars, artisans, and merchants from myriad lands— Greeks, Armenians, Syrians, Jews, and Latins, to name a few. This confluence of cultures fostered an environment where ideas flourished, and intellectual pursuits were highly esteemed.

The Byzantine Empire, with Constantinople as its jewel, was a society deeply rooted in Christian doctrine. The Church played an influential role in daily affairs, guiding everything from political policies to social norms. The Patriarch of Constantinople held immense sway, second only to the Emperor himself. Together, they sought to safeguard the city's spiritual and temporal well-being against the encroaching forces of darkness and discord.

Constantinople served as a vital hub for trade and commerce. Its strategic position between the Black Sea and the Mediterranean made it a natural crossroads for merchants and goods from Asia, Africa, and Europe. The Grand Bazaar and myriad marketplaces bustled with activity, as traders plied their wares—silks from China, spices from India, gems from Persia, and furs from the vast northern forests.

The citizenry of Constantinople relished vibrant public life and artistic expression. The Hippodrome, a colossal arena, was a centerpiece of the city's cultural life, where chariot races, public speeches, and ceremonies took place. The performing arts thrived within this space, with theaters showcasing dramatic plays, poetic recitations, and musical compositions that stirred the soul.

Yet, beneath the veneer of splendor and sophistication, Constantinople was a city often riven by internal strife and external threats. The Byzantine Empire, over centuries, faced relentless assaults from various adversaries —Persians, Arabs, Slavs, and Normans. Each attack left indelible marks, scars that are testimony to both the resilience and vulnerability of this august city.

The societal framework of Constantinople was complex, with a marked hierarchy that delineated the roles and responsibilities of its inhabitants. Nobles and bureaucrats held sway over the administrative machinery, while craftsmen and laborers formed the backbone of its thriving economy. Even within the ecclesiastical sphere, a delineated structure ensured the smooth operation of religious affairs, with monks, priests, and bishops each contributing to the city's spiritual vibrancy.

In the centuries preceding the siege, the population of Constantinople had nurtured a rich tradition of theological scholarship. The various monasteries and educational institutions served as bastions of learning, where men of letters debated the intricacies of Christian doctrine and sought to reconcile faith with reason. Monasticism held a revered place, with holy men dedicating their lives to prayer, contemplation, and the copying of sacred manuscripts.

The city's libraries were repositories of ancient texts, preserving the wisdom of Aristotle, Plato, and other luminaries of the classical world. This intellectual heritage was a source of pride, a reminder of the Byzantine's continuity with the ancient Greco-Roman world. Scribes and scholars labored to maintain this tradition, ensuring that the light of knowledge never dimmed.

Throughout this cultural landscape, one figure rises to paramount significance—Emperor Constantine XI Palaiologos. As the last emperor of Byzantium, Constantine XI embodied the steadfast resolve of his ancestors. His reign, though fraught with peril, was characterized by an unwavering commitment to preserving the dignity and sanctity of Constantinople. Under his stewardship, the city made its final stand, not just as a fortress but as a symbol of an enduring legacy.

A striking feature of Constantinople's culture was its religious art, which adorned every corner of the city. Icons of saints and scenes from the Bible were meticulously crafted, serving both as objects of veneration and as visual theology. Byzantine mosaics, with their resplendent gold backgrounds, depicted divine figures and heavenly visions, bringing solace and inspiration to the faithful who beheld them.

Despite its entrenched Christian identity, Constantinople was not insular. The city had long been a melting pot, where cultures met and mingled. Latin and Greek influences coexisted, sometimes contentiously, within its walls. The Venetians, Genoese, and Pisans, among others, maintained commercial quarters in the city, facilitating a flow of ideas and goods that enriched its cultural fabric.

This bustling, cosmopolitan atmosphere was set against a backdrop of impending doom, as the Ottoman threat loomed ever larger. The fall of Constantinople in 1453 was not merely a conquest; it was a cataclysmic event that marked the end of an era. Yet, even in its twilight, the culture of Constantinople cast a long shadow, influencing the Renaissance and shaping the future of Europe.

As night descends upon this city of splendor and sorrow, the echoes of its last stand reverberate through the annals of history. The Siege of Constantinople was not just a military conflict, but a cultural watershed, a poignant reminder of the resilience and beauty of the human spirit in the face of inexorable change.

Military Strategies Used in the Siege

The Siege of Constantinople witnessed a convergence of military ingenuity and unyielding resolve. Amidst the clashing of blades and the thunderous roar of cannons, the strategies employed bore the mark of both classical warfare and evolving tactical advancements. The Ottomans, under the command of Sultan Mehmed II, designed a siege that would test the mettle of Constantinople's defenders, who fought with the valor akin to the ancient warriors themselves.

One cannot discuss the siege without acknowledging the strategic brilliance of the Ottoman encirclement. Mehmed II, with a keen eye for topography and human psychology, orchestrated a plan that surrounded the city by land and sea. His forces cut off supply lines, creating a blockade meant to starve the defenders into submission. This multifaceted approach leveraged the land-based artillery and naval prowess, a testimony to the Sultan's understanding of combined arms warfare.

At the heart of the Ottoman strategy lay the immense cannons, the likes of which the world had seldom seen. These massive weapons, engineered by the Hungarian master cannon founder, Urban, unleashed destructive power against the city's formidable Theodosian Walls. The continual bombardment sought to break the very backbone of Constantinople's defenses. The thundering echo of the cannons reverberated through the hearts of defenders, shaking the core of Byzantine fortitude.

The defenders, led by Emperor Constantine XI, deployed classic yet effective defensive tactics. They utilized the double line of fortifications, maximizing the depth of their defenses. The inner and outer walls, coupled with the mighty moat, created layers of hurdles for the Ottomans to overcome. Byzantine engineers, with an exceptional understanding of defensive architecture, crafted traps and strategic kill zones to maximize the casualties inflicted upon the attackers.

Tactically astute, Constantine XI and his generals harnessed the city's naval strengths. The Byzantine fleet, though diminished, played a critical role in thwarting Ottoman attempts to completely dominate the waterways. Notably, the great chain across the Golden Horn served as a maritime barricade. This strategic defense impeded the Ottomans from launching a surprise assault from the north, safeguarding a crucial supply route and buying precious time for the city's beleaguered defenders.

Deception played a role as well in the Byzantine strategies. Feigned attacks and sallies aimed to confuse and demoralize the Ottoman troops. These maneuvers, though not always successful, demonstrated the defenders' ability to strike back and maintain some semblance of control over the battlefield. Such actions bolstered morale among the men, reminding them that victory was not solely the province of the aggressors.

Meanwhile, the Ottomans, showing no mercy nor sign of relenting, adopted a shock-and-awe approach. Mehmed II's forces frequently launched night assaults and surprise attacks, designed to exploit the weariness and dwindling numbers of the defenders. The relentless pressure applied by the Ottomans kept the defenders in a constant state of alert, depleting their energies and resources over time.

A pivotal moment in the siege was the transport of Ottoman ships overland into the Golden Horn. A maneuver of both audacity and incredible logistical skill, it demonstrated Mehmed II's willingness to employ unconventional tactics to achieve his objectives. By dragging ships across greased logs over a mile of hilly terrain, the Ottomans effectively bypassed the defensive chain and opened a new front. This brilliant stroke put immense pressure on the already overextended Byzantine defenders.

Throughout this arduous siege, both sides called upon their deep wells of religious and cultural resolve. For the Byzantines, the defense of Constantinople was not merely a military endeavor but a sacred duty. The city's fall would mark an epochal shift, the end of a thousand-year legacy that was both a spiritual stronghold and the heart of Eastern Christendom.

In their final desperate measures, the Byzantines sought foreign aid, sending messages of urgency to potential allies. Unfortunately, geopolitical currents and the spread of the dreaded plague hindered any significant assistance from arriving in time. The failure to muster reinforcements revealed the strategic importance of foresight and comprehensive alliance building, something that future generations would need to remember and heed.

On the Ottoman side, Mehmed's forces were akin to an inexorable tide, fueled by both their martial prowess and a sense of divine mission. The conceptualization and implementation of siege tactics exhibited not just raw might but a calculated and adaptive mindset. The Ottomans demonstrated a mastery of siegecraft that blended brutal force with innovation, an amalgamation of medieval tenacity and the burgeoning Renaissance thinking.

When the final assault came, it was not merely an attack but a crescendo of accumulated tactical expertise. The breaches in the walls, painstakingly created by continuous bombardment, became the portals of destiny through which the Ottoman soldiers poured. In the thick of battle, the ultimate strategy unfolded not just in rigid formations but in the raw chaos of melee combat, where individual acts of bravery and desperation decided the city's fate.

Thus, the Siege of Constantinople stands as a monumental testament to the confluence of strategic brilliance and the indomitable courage of its participants. The military strategies used in the siege encompassed an array of tactics that evolved from the ancient to the modern, reflecting a clash of worlds bearing the weight of history and destiny. The legacy of these strategies would echo through the annals of military history, a somber reminder of both human ingenuity and the perpetual cycle of conflict and conquest.

Chapter 2: The Rise of John Hunyadi

Emerging from the verdant lands of Transylvania, John Hunyadi's ascent to prominence is marked not by mere circumstance but by an indomitable spirit and strategic mind. His early life is etched with rigorous military training and an unyielding pursuit of mastery in the art of war. Amidst the turmoil of a Europe besieged by the Ottoman menace, Hunyadi's initial military campaigns blazed with victories that heralded a new dawn. His cunning on the battlefield and ability to inspire his men transformed him into a beacon of hope for Christendom. It was these early triumphs, fanned by the winds of destiny, that unfurled his voyage towards becoming one of history's most formidable warriors. Thus, John Hunyadi, with sword in hand and faith in heart, embarked upon a journey that would forever alter the course of European history and fortify the bulwarks of Christendom against the Ottoman tide.

Early Life and Military Training

The tale of John Hunyadi's early life unfolds amidst the rolling hills and valiant whispers of a nascent Hungary. Born unto a noble lineage in the year of our Lord fourteen hundred and seven, Hunyadi's youthful days were a canvas painted with shades of provincial nobility and clandestine legend. His father, Voyk, hailing from Wallachian roots, carried within him a legacy that was to be passed down to his son—a legacy of indomitable spirit and tactical acumen.

In the tender years of his youth, young John was reared in the familial estate, where tales of chivalry and honor punctuated his education. The Hunyadi household, though noble, was not untouched by the trials and tribulations that beset their land. Living amidst the thickening threat of conquest and cultural tumult, John imbibed the trials of his forefathers like the very marrow of his bones. His early education was by no means confined to scholarly pursuits alone; he absorbed the tenets of faith, fortitude, and, notably, the martial code. It was here, amid rustic tapestries and hearthside sagas, that the boy first envisioned the hero he was destined to become.

As he grew in both stature and years, John's forays into the world of martial prowess began to take a more defined shape. The courtly circles of Hungary were rife with whispers of grandeur and battle-hardened knights. It is said that even in these fledgling years, his eyes would gleam with dreams of valor and duty. To fortify his burgeoning aspirations, he entrenched himself in the study of classical military strategies and the laws of combat, drawing wisdom from the ancient tomes of Roman and Greek tacticians.

By the time he reached the age of manhood, not a soul questioned John's readiness to don the armor of a warrior. Trails of arduous training, often under the watchful gaze of seasoned knights, heralded his transition from an expectant youth to a figure poised for legendary deeds. He dedicated himself to mastering the longsword, the cavalry shield, and the art of archery—leaving no weapon nor stratagem unlearned in his quest for martial excellence. More than mere skill, it was his unwavering resolve that set him apart, etching his name in the corridors of burgeoning military renown.

John Hunyadi's formative experiences weren't limited to the training grounds and familial tales. Being dispatched to foreign courts as a squire solidified his understanding of the greater geopolitical landscape. These postings not only honed his diplomatic acumen but also exposed him to the complexities of medieval warfare. His service under Sigismund of Luxembourg, the Holy Roman Emperor, provided him with a firsthand glimpse into the machinations of power. These experiences were to become the foundation upon which he built his strategic genius.

The influence of his loyal kin and mentors cannot be overstated. Key to his molding was his knightly tutelage under Filippo Scolari, also known as Pippo Spano, whose valor and shrewd military exploits were heralded across the land. From him, Hunyadi learned the crucial blend of daring and deliberation. This balance of impetuous courage and strategic foresight would later define his command on the battlefield, making him an adversary that armies would come to dread.

It was inevitable that Hungary's complex ties with neighboring realms would test young Hunyadi's mettle. Whether caught in the swirling tides of skirmishes against the Ottoman foe or the internecine conflicts that plagued the region, he began to rise in stature through a series of battle exploits. His innovative tactics, tempered by innate bravery, brought early victories that eclipsed the feats of many seasoned commanders. These fledgling triumphs merely portended the epic encounters that awaited him in the grim chapters of his destiny.

Marriage to Erzsébet Szilágyi further cemented his social standing and drew him deeper into the influential circles of Hungarian nobility. This alliance also provided him with the moral and logistical support necessary to pursue his military ambitions unencumbered. Erzsébet herself was a woman of remarkable strength and virtue, and her unwavering support played a not insignificant role in shaping John's indomitable spirit.

Rising through the ranks with a sense of exigent purpose, Hunyadi's reputation burgeoned as a defender of Christendom. His allegiance to the cross was unwavering, adorned by a zealous desire to protect his realm from the specter of the encroaching Ottoman Empire. Yet, it was not just the clanging of steel and the martial drumming that defined him. The crucible of his early trials fostered a profound spiritual connection, imbuing his every campaign with a sense of divine mission, a celestial calling etched into the very fabric of his soul.

In sum, the early life and military training of John Hunyadi were not merely a prelude to his legend; they were the crucible that forged the steel of his character. From the hearth of his familial estate to the thrilling theaters of martial valor, every experience, every trial, stoked the fire within him. His journey from a young noble lad to a master of military stratagems offers an essential backdrop to his later exploits and unfathomable contributions to the annals of history. Emerging from his early years, ready to wield his sword in both honor and fervor, John Hunyadi stood poised on the brink of remarkable feats, a looming beacon of hope and resistance for the Hungarian realms and Christendom itself.

Initial Military Campaigns and Victories

As the early dawn heralded a new era, John Hunyadi embarked upon a series of martial engagements that would etch his name into the annals of history. His initial campaigns, though nascent in grandeur, displayed a precocious tactical brilliance that belied the years of experience he would later accrue. War, that immutable trial by fire, saw the rise of a leader whose sword glistened with the fire of righteousness and unyielding resolve.

In the shadowy corridors of medieval Europe, where the specter of Ottoman dominion loomed ever large, Hunyadi's early skirmishes were not merely battles but proclamations of defiance. His first few forays into the realm of warfare were against the perennially turbulent Wallachian and Moldavian territories. These lands, steeped in strife and turmoil, witnessed the surgical precision of Hunyadi's military maneuvers. Not one to waste an opportunity, he meticulously honed his strategies, learning from each clash, each parry, and each weary, blood-strewn battlefield. His encounters, victorious though they often were, were fraught with the specter of treachery, a shadow he learned to navigate with cunning and valor.

Thus endowed with the acumen of a seasoned strategist and the bravery of a lionheart, Hunyadi turned his gaze towards the Carpathian passes. These ventures were no less formidable; the mountainous terrain, a formidable adversary by itself, seemed almost to conspire with his human foes. Yet, if mountains dared whisper defiance, his answer came swiftly by the thunderclap of his sword. With each victory, he carved his legend deeper into the heart of Europe. The icy winds of those passes carried tales of his indomitable spirit, echoing through the valleys and beyond.

As fate would ordain, one of Hunyadi's most significant early trials came during the campaigns against the voivodes of Transylvania. These skirmishes were marked by acts of remarkable gallantry and ingenious subterfuge. In the crucible of such encounters, Hunyadi's troops were not just soldiers; they were instruments of a divine symphony, orchestrated by their maestro's unerring command. His adversaries, often left in disarray, could only marvel at the prowess of a man whose hands shaped the destiny of Christendom.

The burgeoning threat from the ever-expanding Ottoman Empire found in Hunyadi a formidable antagonist. In the years leading up to more prominent confrontations, his campaigns against the vanguard of Ottoman incursions demonstrated an uncanny knack for outmaneuvering an enemy that to many seemed insurmountable. Whether by fortifying key castles, launching swift cavalry raids, or deploying innovative siege tactics, his early victories were harbingers of much greater triumphs to come.

Perhaps one of the most emblematic episodes of Hunyadi's rising star was the Battle of Bătălia de la Ialomița. Facing a formidable Turkish vanguard, Hunyadi's forces, though numerically inferior, displayed an unparalleled ferocity and strategic acuity. Through a combination of deceptive retreats and well-executed ambushes, he turned the tide against an opponent thought invincible by many. This battle, a crucible for his nascent strategic genius, showcased the indomitable will that would come to characterize his legacy.

In these early triumphs, one cannot overlook the role played by Hunyadi's loyalty to his men and his unyielding sense of justice. His army, a melting pot of various nationalities, reflected his vision of unity amidst diversity. From Hungarians to Szeklers and even Serbians, his troops were bound not merely by military command but by shared faith and common purpose. Hunyadi's leadership was that of a shepherd guiding his flock through the vale of adversity, unyielding yet benevolent. The echoes of his victories served as clarions, rallying all those who cherished freedom and feared the encroaching shadow of Ottoman rule.

It was no surprise, then, that Hunyadi's name began to resonate beyond the borders of Hungary. To the Pope, lords, and common folk alike, the tales of his early campaigns stirred a sense of hope and urgency. The immense challenge posed by the Ottoman expansion required leaders of exceptional caliber, and in Hunyadi, Christendom recognized a general who could stand as the bulwark against the tide of tyranny.

In these years of relentless warfare and unyielding struggle, Hunyadi's strategies evolved from mere battlefield tactics to comprehensive military doctrines. His emphasis on mobility, the innovative use of fortifications, and the psychological warfare he waged against his enemies set the foundation for his more extensive campaigns. The seeds sown in these initial victories would later bloom into the full military prowess that culminated at the Battle of Belgrade.

Let us consider, at this juncture, Hunyadi not merely as a warrior of flesh and blood but as a symbol of an era's undying spirit. With each fort captured and each enemy vanquished, he wrote an epic not only of military triumph but of a civilization's endurance. His initial campaigns and victories accomplished more than the temporary subjugation of foes; they affirmed a broader narrative of resilience, unity, and faith in the face of overwhelming odds.

With every campaign, with every victory, Hunyadi's reputation spread like wildfire through the embattled lands of Christendom. The dark forests and sweeping plains of Eastern Europe became the canvas upon which he painted his legacy, etching his name alongside the greats of history. These early military engagements, marked by their sheer audacity and tactical brilliance, established Hunyadi not just as a local hero but as a bastion against the impending Ottoman storm.

As the pages of history turn, one reflects upon these early years of John Hunyadi with a sense of awe and reverence. For it is in these initial military campaigns and victories that the seeds of a much grander narrative were sown—a narrative that would see the Battle of Belgrade become a defining moment in the annals of Western civilization. And so, Hunyadi's rise from these humble yet heroic beginnings set the stage for a destiny that would echo through the corridors of time, an enduring testament to the indomitable will of a true crusader.

Thus, with each valiant stride upon the unfriendly terrain of conflict, John Hunyadi braced himself for battles yet to come. His initial campaigns and victories were stepping stones that led, inexorably, to the crescendo that awaited him—the momentous Battle of Belgrade. There, amidst the din of clashing swords and reverent prayers, the full measure of his genius and valor would be revealed, altering the course of history forevermore.

Chapter 3: The Ottoman Threat

The mighty shadows of the Ottoman Empire began their inexorable stretch across the lands, a harbinger of tumult and turbulence for Christendom. In their relentless quest for dominion, the Ottomans mounted campaigns that struck dread amidst the fortresses and parishes of Europe. These fierce warriors, with their scimitars and strategic acumen, pushed against the very ramparts of the known world, challenging the sanctity and sovereignty of the Holy Roman Empire. The initial encounters were marked by clashing steel and the cries of the beleaguered, yet amid this storm stood a bulwark of indomitable spirit— John Hunyadi. With the specter of conquest looming, his valor and strategic brilliance began to illuminate the path to resistance. This nascent menace hinted at the cataclysm that was to come, planting the seeds for a confrontation that would resonate through the annals of history. Hunyadi's unyielding resolve against this Ottoman tide became a beacon of hope, a testament to the enduring spirit of those who dared to stand and fight, and thus the stage was set for the epic saga of Belgrade.

Expansion of the Ottoman Empire

The pages of history are sullied by the looming shadow cast by the Ottomans, an empire burgeoning with ambition that seemed to feast upon the very substance of Christendom. In their relentless advance, they moved like a torrent, unhampered and insatiable. With each conspired conquest, their reaches extended, their dominion multiplied—their ambition, stark, unrelenting.

This monumental expansion was catalyzed by a series of calculated maneuvers on both land and sea. In the early fifteenth century, under the reigns of zealous rulers like Mehmed the Conqueror, the gallant Turks amplified their grip, from Anatolia to the very edges of Europe. They firmly set their sigil upon the once-unyielding fortress of Constantinople, thereby asserting a dominion that inspired dread and admiration alike.

Indeed, the fall of Constantinople in 1453 did not halt their momentum, but rather, it ignited a conflagration that swept through the Balkans, Greece, and beyond. With the fall of such a city—Christendom's bastion—an indomitable spirit seemed to rally within the Ottoman force. The once-impervious walls of Constantinople now became a testament to Ottoman prowess and a lamentation of Christian arrears.

Yet, these conquests were not solely of brute force; craft and stratagem flavored their campaigns. Strategic marriages, cunning diplomacy, and the subtle coquetry of appeasements, all forged the foundations of their extended sovereignty. It is whispered in historical annals that their rise was as much about guile as it was about might. Kings and emperors alike quivered under the weight of Ottoman espionage and intrigue, such dark arts being just as formidable as their scimitars.

Prowl those dusty records, you shall find the Ottomans did not merely rest upon their laurels but always sought further realms to subdue. Territories in Hungary, the Slavonic lands, and even distant Italy found themselves under threat. Fortifications, once believed impervious, crumbled before the ardent despotism of Ottoman generals keen to please their sultan.

In this theater of continual conflict, Serbia bore the brunt of the Turkish ambition, with Macedonian lands also succumbing to the Sultan's grip. These campaigns were fiercely contested. The very heartlands of Southeastern Europe were now a hotbed of activity, battled over and subjugated by the Ottoman blade. Lands once rich with history and culture now found themselves under an unyielding crescent moon.

Among the significant tales of valor that arose during these encroachments was that of the valiant Prince Vlad the Impaler, a figure whose name still conjures images of ghastly resolve and ruthless defense tactics. Though Dracula's legend endures in myth and fiction, his historical resistance was very much palpable. His staunch defiance offered the Ottoman Empire a stark reminder that their path to dominion would not be unchallenged.

John Hunyadi, another luminary figure, stood as a bulwark against this tidal wave of Ottoman expansion. A military commander of unfathomable prowess and astuteness, Hunyadi dedicated much of his existence to repelling the Turks. His name became synonymous with Christian resistance, particularly after his grand stance at the gates of Belgrade. Hunyadi's readiness to combat the Sultan's forces marked a fervent chapter in Europe's defense.

The Siege of Belgrade in 1456, catalyzed by Hunyadi's strategic genius, represents a pinnacle of Christian militancy against this Ottoman expansion. It was no meager confrontation, but a clash that reverberated through all Christendom. The Ottoman ambition aimed to recast Europe under their domination was, at least temporarily, thwarted.

But alas, the imperial insatiability was far from abated. Even after such repulsions, the empire's agents sought newer lands and strategic ports across the Aegean seas and deeper into Eastern Europe. They operated with an uncanny relentlessness, converting Christian churches into mosques, reshaping social fabrics to echo their own cultural mores, embedding their architecture and language upon the vanquished territories.

Their maritime prowess also played a substantial role. Ottoman fleets ruled the Mediterranean waves, their galleys steadfast and invincible. The conquest of islands such as Rhodes and Cyprus echoed this maritime supremacy, stood as bitter reminders of an empire unburdened by the limitations that once held feudal realms shackled to the land.

Perish the thought that Europe remained idle; myriad coalitions and alliances were forged and fueled by the carnage of Ottoman advances. The Holy League, with inputs from Venice, Spain, and the Papal States, all sought to reclaim the lands drenched in Christian blood. These efforts, combined with internal strife within the Ottoman ranks, occasionally compelled the empire to retreat or recalibrate.

The Janissaries, an elite corps, became emblematic of the empire's reach. Born of Christian conscripts, these troops were converted, trained, and turned into soldiers of the Sultan—a macabre irony if ever there was one. They were the mailed fist of the Ottoman might, both feared and revered, intricately woven into the fabric of the empire's military machine.

As we pierce deeper into the annals, one discerns that the roots of this expansion were as much economic as they were militant. Conquered lands were bled for tributes, and the spoils of war enriched the Sultan's coffers. Trade routes were recalibrated to serve the Ottoman advantage, while artisans and traders were absorbed into the empire's vast commercial networks.

This inexorable spread characterized by quelling revolts, sacking cities, and subduing realms, broadened their dominion from Bosnia to the very thresholds of Vienna. These acts augment unfolding narratives with ample evidence of the Ottomans' sweeping significance across the vast canvas of history.

However, this tide would find some able to stand, and against this near-endless advance, heroes like Hunyadi arose, luminous in their defiance and resolve. The collective memory assiduously maintained by Rome, the defiance of their steel-clad warriors, and the fortitude of resolute leaders created pockets of resistance that the Ottoman juggernaut found insurmountable at times.

Thus, as the chronicles reveal, the expansion of the Ottoman Empire was a multifaceted marvel—a confluence of military brilliance, astute diplomacy, and economic stratification. An empire born in the crucible of ambition, tempered by conquests, and etched in the annals of time as both a force revered and feared.

Initial Encounters with the Ottomans

The Pale of the Magyars first felt the grim whispers of the Ottoman menace in the early years of the fifteenth century. Like the foreboding shadows of an approaching storm, the Ottomans' encroachment into European lands signaled an unholy tempest. Fear and foreboding spread through the valleys and over the ramparts of Christian fortifications, bringing tales of the invincible Osmanlis who swept across the Balkans with a ruthless efficiency.

In these early encounters, the clash between the Ottoman forces and the Hungarian defenders rang loudest. The Hungarians, under the nascent but formidable leadership of John Hunyadi, clashed with Ottoman raiding parties that dared to breach the sanctity of their borders. Hunyadi, still carving his place in the annals of history, found his mettle tested against an enemy like none other he had faced before.

Amongst the myriad skirmishes, the Battle of Kunovica in 1444 stands out as a pivotal moment. Here, Hunyadi employed a blend of strategic cunning and valor, delivering the Ottomans a rare but biting defeat. This encounter demonstrated his military acumen, which lay not in sheer force but in the deft execution of cunning stratagems. His methods became legend, and his name resonated through Hungarian lands and beyond, a harbinger of hope in dark times.

Yet, each victory came at great cost. The clash with the Ottomans exacted a heavy toll on men and resources, and the relentless marches of Ottoman forces stretched the Hungarian defenses to their limits. It became evident that these were not mere skirmishes but part of a grander design, an incessant press against the bastions of Christendom.

The Hungarian morale, however, remained undaunted. Despite the specter of Ottoman vengeance looming ever larger, Hunyadi and his followers held their ground with unyielding resolve. The call to arms echoed through the ranks, for Christian Europe mustered every ounce of determination to repel this new adversary. Yet, it was in these early thrusts and parries that both sides learned of each other's strengths, weaknesses, and, most importantly, the limits of human endurance.

As Hunyadi's reputation burgeoned, so did the gravity of his encounters. The Ottomans were not a foe content with small victories; their ambition lay in the heart of Europe. With every clash, they tested the resolve of the Christian world, seeking cracks in its armor. Hunyadi, prescient and vigilant, understood that mere defense would not suffice. Offensive maneuvers, unexpected and forceful, became his hallmark, as he strove to blunt the Ottoman's relentless advance.

Tensions escalated as the 1440s drew to a close, with the Ottomans launching increasingly audacious campaigns. Hunyadi, now the recognized defender of Christendom, found himself in the unenviable position of having to predict and preempt the Sultan's every move. Intelligence became as valuable as weaponry, and cunning as crucial as valor.

It is worth noting that these early encounters were not just about Hunyadi versus the Ottomans; they were a crucible forging an alliance of European states wary of the Turkish yoke. The Ottomans' campaigns prompted Christian princes and kings to reevaluate strategies, form alliances, and empower leaders like Hunyadi who could stand against the advancing tide.

In the years leading up to the infamous Siege of Belgrade, the initial encounters with the Ottomans served as the proving grounds for Hunyadi's tactics and leadership. Each battle imbued Hunyadi with greater insight into the Ottoman war machine. The sieges and clashes were not mere military engagements but a series of lessons from which a grand strategy against the Turks would emerge.

Despite the destruction and chaos wrought by these initial encounters, there were important silver linings. The early clashes revealed the weaknesses of the Ottoman military structure, particularly its reliance on rapid mobility and feigned retreats, akin to the ancient Parthian tactics. Hunyadi's brilliance lay in his ability to turn these weaknesses to his advantage, setting traps and ambushes that confounded his opponents.

But beyond the tactics and the strategies, these first encounters also kindled a spark of resistance within the broader Christian populace. The tales of Hunyadi's grit, the valor of Hungarian soldiers, and the righteous struggle against the foreign invader were carried far and wide, turning fear into fervor. This was not merely a conflict of swords and shields; it was a clash of civilizations, a righteous defense of the Christian faith against the encroachments of Islam.

In the grand theater of the epoch, these initial encounters served as the ominous prelude to the monumental events that were yet to come. Every skirmish, raid, and battle was a step towards the greater conflict, painting the landscape of the struggle with hues of blood, valor, and divine purpose. The shadow of the Crescent waxed and waned, testing the resilience of the Cross, and setting the stage for the epic confrontations that would define Europe's destiny.

Chapter 4: The Role of Pope Callixtus III

In those tumultuous times, upon the delicate tapestry of Christendom, there emerged the resolute figure of Pope Callixtus III, whose papal mandate transcended ecclesiastical boundaries to etch an indelible mark upon the annals of history. Confronted with the relentless advance of the Ottoman horde, the Holy Father, with a fervor unmatched, promulgated a rallying call to all Christian nations, summoning the faithful to defend the bulwarks of their sacred heritage. His decree for the tolling of noon bells, resonating through the spires and bell towers of Europe, was an invocation to unity and divine intervention, beseeching the Lord's grace upon those valiant souls who girded themselves for the imminent clash at Belgrade. Pope Callixtus III's involvement was not merely as a shepherd tending his flock but as a stalwart captain, whose spiritual and moral leadership underpinned the Christian armies' resolve, binding them in a covenant of faith as they stood upon the precipice of destiny.

Papal Policies and Influence

The epoch of Pope Callixtus III was one of immense turmoil and formidable challenge, as the Ottoman specter cast a long and sinister shadow over Christian Europe. Thrust into the papal robe in 1455, Callixtus III was burdened with the colossal mandate of curbing the Ottoman tide. His policies, steeped in fervor and conviction, were instrumental in galvanizing Christendom to unite against the infidel forces of Sultan Mehmed II.

Pope Callixtus III, born Alfonso de Borgia, was no stranger to the stratagems of governance and diplomacy. Before ascending to the pontifical throne, he had served as a cardinal and was well-versed in the art of negotiation and ecclesiastical administration. It was by no mere happenstance that his papacy coincided with one of the most pivotal junctures in the history of Christendom. His policies were deeply intertwined with the prevailing need to forestall the Ottoman invasion and to fortify Christian strongholds.

The Pope's first significant decree was the Bull of Crusade, a clarion call to all Christian princes and subjects to take up arms against the Ottoman threat. Callixtus III exuded an aura of unwavering determination as he rallied the Christian states. His missives, adorned with the papal seal, resonated with the exhortation to defend the sanctity of Europe. The Bull of Crusade was not merely a call to arms; it was an invocation of divine duty, appealing to both the martial and spiritual sensibilities of his audience.

At the heart of Callixtus III's policies was the revival of the crusading spirit that had once invigorated Europe. He marshaled the church's considerable resources toward the war effort. Canonical treasures were melted down to mint gold florins, which were then dispatched to fund the Christian armies. Furthermore, the Pope restructured ecclesiastical taxes, redirecting them towards the crusade. His reforms included the levying of a tithe from all clerical incomes, ensuring that the full weight of Christendom's wealth supported the righteous cause.

To further bolster the anti-Ottoman coalition, Callixtus III employed his formidable diplomatic acumen. He embarked on tireless efforts to reconcile warring Christian factions and forge a united front. Diplomatic legations were sent across the dominions of Europe, each bearing the Pope's entreaties and projections of a shared peril. The Christian nations, though divided by politics and personal enmities, found in Callixtus III's missives a common purpose that transcended their parochial interests.

One of the Pope's pivotal triumphs in policy-making was the establishment of a network of correspondence that transcended the farthest reaches of Christendom, uniting lords, kings, and commoners under a singular banner. The missives and decrees sent by Callixtus III carried the weight of celestial endorsement. The pontifical court became a hub of communication, and the Pope's envoys ensured that his directives reverberated through the length and breadth of Europe.

The zeal of Callixtus III was not confined to missives and taxes. Rituals of piety and symbols of unity were also woven into the fabric of his policies. One such significant decree was the institution of the noon bell tolling, an echoing reminder of the peril faced by Christendom and an invocation for divine intercession. Wherever the bells of Christendom tolled at noon, they rekindled the spirits of the faithful, infusing them with a collective resolve. The Pope's piety was thus interlaced with pragmatic measures, seeping into the daily lives of Christians across Europe.

Pope Callixtus III's policies extended beyond the battlefield. He understood the importance of morale and faith in sustaining the war effort. To this end, he canonized saints who epitomized the virtues of courage and sacrifice, such as St. Vincent Ferrer. These canonizations served to kindle the spirits of the faithful, imparting a divine precedent and an exemplar of holy fortitude that was to be emulated in the struggle against the Ottomans.

Moreover, Callixtus III's influence was felt deeply in the realms of ecclesiastical law and administration. His pontificate saw the promulgation of statutes designed to enhance the efficiency and responsiveness of ecclesiastical courts. This legal reinforcement was crucial, as it ensured that the church could swiftly and effectively mobilize resources and adjudicate matters pertaining to the crusade.

As the battle loomed near, Pope Callixtus III's policies also took on a spiritual dimension. He called for days of fasting, prayer, and penance, urging Christians to seek divine favor. Churches across Europe thrummed with the fervent prayers of the faithful, petitions for protection and victory against the Ottoman menace. These spiritual initiatives created a palpable sense of community and shared purpose, uniting disparate groups under the banner of Christendom.

The ramifications of Callixtus III's policies were wrought in the crucible of war at the Battle of Belgrade in 1456. The steadfast leadership and unyielding faith espoused by the Pope had a resounding impact on Christian morale and unity. John Hunyadi, the formidable Hungarian leader, and his forces were emboldened by the unwavering support of the pontiff. The decisive victory at Belgrade, celebrated as a triumph of the divine over earthly might, bore testament to the Pope's influential policies.

In retrospect, the legacy of Pope Callixtus III's policies extends beyond the immediate conflict. His actions laid the groundwork for future papal endeavors in times of crises. The integration of faith and pragmatism in his policies provided a blueprint for the church's role in worldly affairs. Callixtus III's papacy exemplified how spiritual leadership could be interwoven with temporal strategies, inspiring unity and resilience in moments of great peril.

The potent combination of faith, diplomacy, and military support orchestrated by Pope Callixtus III resonates through the annals of history. His policies demonstrated the profound influence of papal authority and the inexorable power of a united Christendom. By forging a collective identity and purpose, Callixtus III ensured that the flames of hope and resistance burned brightly, guiding Christian Europe through its darkest hour. The papal mantle was wielded as both shield and sword, safeguarding the sanctity of Christendom and inscribing Callixtus III's name indelibly in the tapestry of history.

The Decree for Noon Bells

Pope Callixtus III, a figure of divine fate intertwined with temporal affairs, was resolute in his efforts to unify Christendom against the encroaching Ottoman threat. The pontiff's determination to marshal all tools at his disposal was nowhere more evident than in the issuance of the Decree for Noon Bells. This decree, rooted in faith and strategic acumen, sought to bind Christian communities across Europe in a daily act of solidarity and prayer.

The origins of this decree trace back to the fervent year of 1456, a time when the Christian world trembled beneath the formidable shadow of the advancing Ottoman forces. The Turkish host, led by Sultan Mehmed II, had already claimed the venerable city of Constantinople, causing a ripple of dread throughout Europe. Against this backdrop, Pope Callixtus III sought a powerful yet simple unifying act to bolster morale and invite divine favor upon the armies defending the realm of Christendom.

It was decreed that every bell in Christendom should toll at the stroke of noon. This sonorous ritual was not merely a call to prayer but a clarion signal to unite the hearts and minds of the diverse peoples under the Christian banner. The pontiff's intentions were twofold: to invoke divine intervention through collective prayer and to serve as an audible reminder of the omnipresent threat poised at the gates of their world.

As the bells tolled, communities from the verdant hills of Tuscany to the bustling streets of Paris paused in their daily labors. A sanctified silence would follow the resounding peals, as heads bowed and lips murmured supplications for the defenders of Belgrade. This daily reverence was aimed at fostering a spirit of unity and resilience, instilling within the faithful a sense of shared purpose against the Ottoman peril.

Through this decree, Pope Callixtus III ingeniously merged the sacred with the martial. By encouraging synchronous prayers, he not only fortified the spiritual resolve of the people but also communicated a potent message of resistance and defiance to the enemy. The continuous ringing of the bells, like a heartbeat of a united Christendom, reverberated across mountains, valleys, and rivers, stitching together disparate lands with the thread of shared faith and hope.

Yet this decree was also a testament to the strategic acumen of the pontiff. The noon bells served as a form of psychological warfare, signaling to the Ottomans that Europe remained vigiland undivided in its determination to repel the invaders. Every peal was a declaration that the fight for Christian lands and values was far from over. It was a daily proclamation of unity that echoed across both the physical and spiritual realms, reinforcing the resolve of soldiers and civilians alike.

In the months leading up to the decisive confrontation at Belgrade, the relentless tolling of the noon bells became a familiar echo throughout Europe. This daily observance not only bolstered spiritual fortitude but also strengthened the communal bonds among the disparate Christian territories. Farmers in England, merchants in Venice, and artisans in Flanders were united under the banner of shared faith and common cause, creating a network of support that transcended geographical and political boundaries.

The Decree for Noon Bells exemplified the profound ability of Pope Callixtus III to harness the spiritual energies of his flock and direct them towards a critical earthly endeavor. By calling upon the faithful to participate in this daily rite, he effectively wove a tapestry of collective prayer, each thread fortifying the defense of Christendom. The harmonious resonance of bells served as a tangible reminder of the ever-present struggle and the unwavering need for divine intervention.

Indeed, the miraculous course of the Battle of Belgrade, where the Christian forces triumphed against overwhelming odds, was perceived as a testament to the efficacy of this unifying decree. The victory was not solely attributed to military prowess but was seen as the fruit of piety, galvanized by the combined prayers of thousands. The tolling of the bells had not merely been a ritual; it had been an invocation of divine providence, a calling upon the celestial forces to intercede on behalf of the beleaguered warriors of Belgrade.

In the aftermath of the battle, the Decree for Noon Bells continued to echo across Europe, transforming from a wartime necessity into a cherished tradition. It became a salient reminder of the power of collective prayer and the enduring strength of a united Christian front. The decree's legacy lived on, symbolizing the victorious defense against tyranny, the triumph of faith, and the enduring spirit of unity that could withstand even the most dire of threats.

The decree also had a lasting impact on the cultural landscape of Europe. It became a symbol of resistance and resilience, imbuing the daily lives of the faithful with a renewed sense of purpose and connection. The bells' tolling served as a constant affirmation of the community's shared values and common destiny, fostering a spirit of camaraderie and mutual support that transcended the immediate crisis.

Thus, the Decree for Noon Bells crafted by Pope Callixtus III stands as a monument to the profound interplay between faith and strategy. It highlighted the pontiff's adeptness in utilizing spiritual devotion as a means to rally and unify a diverse continent in the face of existential peril. Through the resonance of the noon bells, the heartbeat of Europe synchronized, forging an unbreakable bond of faith and fortitude that ultimately played a pivotal role in the salvation of Christendom.

So endured the legacy of this decree. Each midday bell, a testament to unity and divine supplication, continues to echo through the ages, reminding posterity of the indomitable spirit that arose in response to the clarion call of Pope Callixtus III. The decree's vibratory might reinforced not only the walls of Belgrade but also the spiritual ramparts guarding the essence of Christian Europe, bespeaking an era wherein mortal and celestial efforts were in harmonious accord.

Chapter 5: Strategic Preparations for Battle

In those harrowing days preceding the tumultuous clash at Belgrade's gates, John Hunyadi, with the resolve of a seasoned tactician and the heart of a lion, embarked on a series of precise and calculated arrangements. His reforms in martial drill and mustering were nothing short of meticulous, transforming raw recruits into hallowed defenders. With valor and sagacity, he forged ironclad alliances through diplomatic discourse, uniting disparate factions under a singular banner against the burgeoning Ottoman threat. The amassing of provisions, the sharpening of blade and wit alike, foreshadowed an epic confrontation. Amidst such fervent preparation, hope mingled with the fervor of faith, as men readied themselves to stand against a tide that threatened Christendom itself. Each stratagem and maneuver crafted by Hunyadi bespoke not only martial promise but the very essence of a divine mission ordained by the heavens.

Hunyadi's Military Reforms

Under the looming shadow of Ottoman expansion, John Hunyadi, the fearless hero of Christendom, embarked on a series of groundbreaking military reforms. His actions were not mere whims of a battle-hardened warrior; they were calculated maneuvers crafted with the diligence of a master strategist. The heart of his reforms lay in creating a disciplined and versatile fighting force, capable of countering the multifaceted threats posed by the Ottoman Empire.

Foremost among his reforms was the reorganization of his army, blending traditional cavalry units with a more reliable and disciplined infantry. The Knights and nobility, clad in their shimmering armor, had long dominated European warfare. However, Hunyadi saw the need for a balanced force. He thus emphasized the training and equipping of infantry units, ensuring they were not only prepared for siege warfare but also capable of holding their ground in open battle.

Hunyadi's genius shone through in his fusion of old and new. He drew from the past the philosophies and tactics that had proven effective while introducing innovative methods to revolutionize his troops' capabilities. His reforms extended beyond the battlefield, permeating the everyday lives of his soldiers. Rigorous training regimens were established, encompassing a variety of combat scenarios. Each soldier was drilled, not only in fighting but in the art of surviving the tumultuous whirl of battle.

The infantry units comprised mainly of peasants, who, under Hunyadi's strict yet fair leadership, were transformed into a formidable fighting force. They were armed with pikes and crossbows, weapons that contrasted sharply with the traditional swords and shields. This shift in armament was part of a broader strategy to enhance the army's flexibility and resilience. By empowering the common soldier, Hunyadi forged a new kind of warrior, less reliant on valor and martial prowess and more on discipline and coordinated effort.

Moreover, Hunyadi didn't neglect the importance of logistics—a facet often underestimated yet crucial for sustained military campaigns. He established robust supply lines, ensuring that his men were well-equipped and well-fed, irrespective of the terrain or distance from friendly territories. This meticulous attention to logistics allowed his forces to endure prolonged engagements, a necessity when facing the seemingly inexhaustible resources of the Ottomans.

Central to Hunyadi's reforms was the establishment of a spy network. Intelligence gathering became indispensable in his strategy to outmaneuver the Ottomans. Through spies and scouts, he acquired critical information about enemy movements, strength, and plans. This foresight enabled him to craft strategies that not only countered imminent threats but also anticipated future challenges. His use of espionage undermined the Ottoman's advantage of vast numbers by striking decisively at opportune moments.

Beyond the tangible changes in equipment and tactics, Hunyadi instilled a profound sense of unity and purpose in his army. His leadership was not merely of authority but of inspiration. He invoked the plight of Christendom, the sacred duty to protect their lands and faith from the looming Crescent. This spiritual and emotional rallying cry fostered unparalleled camaraderie and dedication among his soldiers. They were not merely fighting a war; they were defending their faith, homes, and families.

Another hallmark of Hunyadi's reforms was his adept use of fortifications. Realizing the strategic importance of well-defended strongholds, he oversaw the construction and reinforcement of castles and forts along key border areas. These bastions served as critical points of defense and refuge, thwarting enemy advances and providing his forces with secure bases of operation. His skilled use of fortifications effectively blunted the otherwise overwhelming might of the Ottoman forces.

Hunyadi's understanding of psychological warfare cannot be understated. He often used feigned retreats and ambush tactics to bewilder and demoralize his enemies. These strategies, while simple, required meticulous planning and execution, which his well-trained soldiers performed with precision. The sight of a disciplined force retreating in perfect order, only to reappear in ambush, struck fear and confusion into the hearts of their enemies, turning many battles in Hunyadi's favor.

Perhaps the most defining aspect of Hunyadi's reforms was the integration of foreign elements into his army. Recognizing the value of experienced fighters, he welcomed mercenaries and volunteer soldiers from different regions of Europe. These warriors brought with them diverse combat techniques and knowledge, which Hunyadi adeptly integrated into his strategies. This inclusiveness not only broadened his tactical repertoire but also symbolized the pan-European support for the Christian cause.

Diplomacy also played a crucial role in Hunyadi's overall strategic framework. His military reforms were often accompanied by diplomatic maneuvers designed to secure alliances and support. He worked tirelessly to garner the backing of various European powers, persuading them of the necessity to unite against the common Ottoman threat. These alliances sometimes provided him with crucial reinforcements and resources, bolstering his own formidable forces.

Hunyadi's meticulous attention to detail extended to the battlefield's smallest elements. He ensured that each unit had a clear line of communication, employing signal systems that allowed coherent and swift movement orders. His commanders were trained to make rapid decisions, adapting strategies as the battle unfurled. This dynamic and adaptable command structure allowed his forces to remain cohesive and responsive, even amid the chaos of conflict.

Hunyadi's reforms also included a focus on morale and welfare. Recognizing that a well-treated army is a loyal and effective one, he implemented measures to ensure his soldiers' well-being. These measures included fair distribution of spoils, adequate resting periods, and care for the wounded. His attention to his soldiers' morale won their unwavering loyalty and dedication, strengthening the resolve and cohesion of his forces.

The fruits of Hunyadi's military reforms became vividly apparent in the epic Defense of Belgrade. His army, forged through rigorous discipline and strategic innovation, stood against the fearsome might of Sultan Mehmed II. The fortifications held, the spies conveyed crucial intelligence, and the combined arms of cavalry, infantry, and artillery executed their roles with unparalleled precision. The outcome was a miraculous victory, a testament to Hunyadi's strategic foresight and unwavering dedication to his reforms.

In conclusion, John Hunyadi's military reforms were a tapestry of innovation, discipline, and strategic brilliance. They transformed a fragmented and oft-ill-prepared force into a unified, formidable army, capable of standing against one of the most powerful empires of the time. His reforms transcended the battlefield, reflecting his deep understanding of logistics, intelligence, morale, and the human spirit. These changes did not merely prepare his forces for a single battle; they laid the groundwork for a legacy that would inspire and protect Christendom for generations to come.

Diplomatic Efforts and Alliances

In days yore, wherein valor and cunning oft conspired to shape the fate of nations, John Hunyadi embarked upon a path not solely of swords and shields, but of words and alliances. In preparing for the imminent clash with the Ottoman host, he recognized the profound necessity of diplomacy as a weapon equal to, if not surpassing, the mightiest of blades. Thus, under the looming shadow of conflict, Hunyadi wove a tapestry of alliances and negotiations, each thread a vital component of his grand strategy.

With foresight gleaned from years of skirmishes and conquests, Hunyadi sought the favor of the papacy. His emissaries, bearing both gifts and gravitas, petitioned Pope Callixtus III for support. The Holy See, perceiving the gravity of the Ottoman menace, did not turn a deaf ear. Instead, the papal decree resounded across Christendom, urging the faithful to unite in the holy cause. This entreaty was no mere gesture, but a clarion call that reverberated through abbeys and cathedrals alike, binding the spiritual lifeblood of Europe to Hunyadi's cause.

Beyond the hallowed halls of Rome, Hunyadi's envoys traversed the courts of Europe, beseeching monarchs and princes to join him in defiance of the crescent moon. Some rulers, wary of the Ottoman advance, offered pledges of men and material. Others, ensnared by internecine disputes or cautious of further embroilments, hesitated yet could not completely ignore the rising tide. Promises were extracted by means both fair and cunning, for Hunyadi understood that unity in purpose oft springs from a multitude of motives.

Of particular note were the alliances with the Poles and the Serbs. The bonds forged with these neighboring nations were of the utmost import, not only due to geographic proximity but also shared enmity against the Turkish incursion. Poland, under the guidance of its astute king, dispatched troops and provisions, knowing well that the fall of Hungary would presage their own peril. Serbian princes, too, lent their strength, for the Ottomans' inexorable march had already darkened the borders of their dominions.

Nor should one overlook the endeavors to rally the Dalmatian cities. Nestled along the Adriatic Sea, these maritime strongholds operated as pivotal bastions of trade and defense. Hunyadi recognized their value, not only for their naval capabilities but also for their wealth and fortitude. Diplomatic overtures with Venice and Ragusa sought to secure naval reinforcements, and in return, assurances of commerce and mutual defense were tendered. These cities, ever pragmatic, saw in this accord a bulwark against the expanding Ottoman fleet.

As summer 1456 loomed, emissaries bore urgent dispatches across Europe, seeking mercenaries well-versed in the arts of war. Swiss pikemen, German landsknechts, and Italian condottieri answered the call. These hardened warriors, drawn by coin and cause, lent their blades to Hunyadi, diversifying the martial prowess arrayed against the Sultan's forces. Their inclusion exemplified the transnational character of the Christian resistance, a mosaic of tongues and tactics united under a singular banner.

Yet, cooperation was not an inevitability; rather, it was coaxed and cajoled, embroiled in the politics of the day. The Holy Roman Emperor Frederick III, whose influence spanned vast territories, required delicate handling. Though oft indifferent to Hungarian plights, the encroaching Turk presented a threat too large to ignore. Diplomatic parleys with the Emperor were as much strategic chess games as acts of entreaty, revealing Hunyadi's adeptness in the finesse required to balance imperial ego and existential necessity.

Concurrently, Hunyadi's correspondence with the aristocracy and clergy of Hungary revealed his political savvy. The barons and bishops, wielders of local power and opinion, were persuaded through letters and councils. It was here that Hunyadi's statesmanship shone brightly, for he fostered a nationalistic spirit that transcended regional loyalties. He aligned their interests with the defense of Christendom at large, making it not merely a Hungarian struggle but a crusade to preserve the very essence of their way of life.

To galvanize internal support, Hunyadi invoked a fervor rooted in faith and fear. Sermons resounded from pulpits, extolling the righteousness of the cause and the dire consequences of failure. The people, impelled by the duality of divine favor and existential dread, rallied to the banner of their charismatic leader. In this, the power of rhetoric mingled seamlessly with the integrity of conviction, creating a groundswell of communal resolve.

The recruitment of allies did not cease with nobility and nations. Within the very demesne of Hungary, Hunyadi engaged the peasantry and townsfolk, promising protection and sharing the spoils of war. This multi-layered approach to diplomacy, wherein even the commoner found a voice, fostered a comprehensive mobilization rarely witnessed in history. Such integration of the populace into the strategic framework underscored Hunyadi's foresight and unparalleled ability to unify disparate factions.

Even beyond Christian dominions, Hunyadi sought to exploit the shifting allegiances within the Ottoman sphere. Relationships with dissenting factions and rival claimants to the Sultan's throne were cautiously cultivated. Though shrouded in secrecy, these maneuvers aimed to divide Ottoman unity from within, creating fissures that could be leveraged on the battlefield. Espionage and nuanced diplomacy thus intertwined, creating opportunities that martial prowess alone could not achieve.

In truth, the diplomatic efforts and alliances arranged by John Hunyadi were as intricate and formidable as any battle plan. He wove a web that spanned cities and courts, connecting diverse entities in a collective struggle against a common foe. Each alliance bore unique stipulations and demands, yet all were bound by the zealous aim to thwart the Ottoman tide. Therefore, as the impending Battle of Belgrade drew near, it was not merely the clashing of steel that would determine its outcome, but the cumulative strength of a united Christendom, meticulously orchestrated by Hunyadi's diplomatic genius.

Chapter 6: The Battle of Belgrade

The sun crested over the horizon, heralding the dawn of that fateful day in July 1456, as John Hunyadi and his valiant forces stood poised to engage the might of the Ottoman Empire. With hearts aflame and spirits undeterred, they embraced the looming clash against Sultan Mehmed II's formidable army. The air thickened with tension, every breath steeped in anticipation. Hunyadi, a master of battlefield tactics, orchestrated his men with unwavering precision. Waves of Hungarian warriors clashed ferociously against Ottoman ranks, each clash of steel echoing the conviction of their cause. Amidst the tumult, a pivotal moment arrived; a daring sortie led by Hunyadi himself pierced the enemy's heart, turning the tide. As the night descended, the shattered remnants of the Ottoman forces retreated, bearing testimony to the audacious bravery and strategic genius that had secured Christendom's bulwark. The victory at Belgrade, achieved through divine favor and indomitable will, became a beacon of hope and unity across Europe, etching Hunyadi's name in the annals of history as a savior and stalwart defender of the faith.

Battlefield Tactics and Movements

As dawn broke over the fields of Belgrade, two great armies stood poised, each driven by fires of fervent conviction and the unyielding resolve to vanquish the other. The Battle of Belgrade, much like the strategic dance of sinew and steel, saw the choreography of tactical genius, a relentless pursuit of dominion, and a series of movements executed with unparalleled precision.

John Hunyadi, the captain-general of Hungary and a master of warfare, marshaled his forces with the adeptness of a seasoned commander. The battlefield, a theater of imminent clash, was mapped out in his mind like a grand chessboard. He had arranged his infantry and cavalry in formations that maximized both defensive stability and offensive prowess. His foresight was evident as he positioned archers and artillery at vantage points, ensuring that the enemy could not advance unscathed.

The Ottomans, under the command of Sultan Mehmed II, were no less resourceful. They approached with a formidable array of Janissaries, spearmen, and cavalry, each segment honed to perfection through years of conquest. Their initial movements aimed at breaching the walls of Belgrade, a fortress deemed impenetrable.

The battle commenced with the clash of vanguard forces, the thunderous roar of cannons, and the airy whistle of arrows raining from the heavens. Commanders on both sides orchestrated their units like maestros, adapting and reacting to the undulating tide of combat. Hunyadi's knights, adorned in plate armor and wielding lances, surged forth in disciplined charges, their momentum a sledgehammer against the Ottoman lines.

Notable among Hunyadi's tactics was his adept use of feigned retreats, a stratagem that lured the Ottomans into traps laid by the Hungarian forces. This cunning maneuver caused disarray among the Sultan's ranks, leaving them susceptible to counterattacks. As one cohort fell back, another was prepared to surge forward and exploit the momentary confusion.

Amid the chaos, Hunyadi demonstrated an impeccable sense of timing and resourcefulness. Dispatching swift messengers, he communicated his commands across the various fronts, coordinating intricate movements that brought unity to his disparate forces. While the Sultan's forces often relied on brute force and size, Hunyadi harnessed the power of strategic acumen and a tenacious spirit.

The pivotal moment came when Hunyadi deployed his reserve forces, the core of his strategic depth. This disciplined and rested contingent surged like a tempest, breaking through the Ottoman center. The horses' gallop resonated like the drums of war, instilling both hope and fear. With sword and shield, they carved a path through the enemy, leaving a trail of valor behind.

In a dramatic twist, Hunyadi himself took to the field, donned in battle armor and brandishing a sword that gleamed in the sunlight. His presence invigorated his troops, turning the tide as they rallied to his banner. The battlefield, once a scene of organized chaos, now reflected the will of a leader undeterred by the specter of defeat.

The Ottomans, though resilient, found their formations buckling under the relentless Hungarian assaults. Their attempts to regroup were thwarted by Hunyadi's constant pressure and the mobility of his light cavalry. These riders, skilled in the art of hit-and-run tactics, disrupted enemy lines and isolated their units, making it difficult for the Ottomans to mount a coordinated defense.

Amidst the din of battle, the clergy and faithful of Belgrade took to the walls of the city, their prayers ascending as a plea for divine favor. It was said that the bell tolls, ordered by Pope Callixtus III, echoed like celestial commands, imbuing the defenders with newfound strength. Whether by mortal means or divine intervention, the tide was turning irreversibly in Hunyadi's favor.

Hunyadi's deployment of defensive formations, such as the "Wagenburg" (a wagon fort), illustrated his strategic ingenuity. This mobile fortress provided a bulwark against the heavy cavalry charges of the Ottomans. The interlocked wagons, bristling with spears and defended by archers, created an impregnable shield, disrupting the momentum of the enemy's mounted units.

The battle raged on with valor and bloodshed underscoring every skirmish. Numerous were the acts of heroism and gallantry, not least from Hunyadi's own circle of knights and commanders. The unity of purpose within the Hungarian ranks contrasted starkly with the fragmented efforts of their foes, whose leadership struggled to maintain cohesion in the face of relentless pressure.

As dusk fell and the clangor of swords began to wane, it became apparent that the Ottomans were faltering. The battlefield bore witness to the extraordinary resolve of Hunyadi's forces, holding the line with indomitable spirit. The Sultan's attempts to rally his troops were in vain. Exhausted and demoralized, they began to yield ground rapidly.

When final reprieve came, it was not solely through the sword but through the inspired leadership and intricate tactics of John Hunyadi, whose name would be etched in history as the savior of Christendom at Belgrade. His mastery over the battlefield, an exhibition of both mind and might, had wrought a victory that reverberated far beyond the immediate conflict.

The significance of this battle extended well beyond the tactical triumphs. It was a moment that symbolized the resilience of Christian Europe in the face of an encroaching empire. The tactical prowess demonstrated by Hunyadi and his forces showcased the ingenuity and indomitable spirit that defined the era's military confrontations.

This episode in the annals of history serves not only as a testament to the skills of warriors but also as a narrative underscored by the resolve to defend faith and homeland. The movements on the battlefield, each step and maneuver calculated with precision, culminated in a victory that was as strategic as it was miraculous, shaping the destiny of nations and the course of European history itself.

Thus, the Battle of Belgrade stands, not merely as a confrontation of arms and armor but as a profound narrative of tactical brilliance, leadership, and unwavering resolve. Within the dust and din of combat, the echoes of Hunyadi's strategies resonate, memorializing a moment where the tides of war were turned by the sheer genius and courage of a singular leader.

Key Moments and Turning Points

The siege was fierce, the stakes perilously high. From the dawn of July 21, 1456, under the glaring sun, two titanic forces clashed at the city walls of Belgrade. Each swing of the sword and each clang of the shield heralded the coming of significant and fateful moments. One such pivotal moment unfolded when John Hunyadi, astute and unyielding, orchestrated a daring counter-assault against the Ottoman besiegers. With resolute courage, his cavalry broke through the enemy's lines, engendering chaos in the Sultan's well-oiled war machine.

The night, however, brought with it another profound turning point. As the moon cast its silver hue upon the battlefield, Hunyadi's forces engaged in a covert operation to dismantle the Ottoman artillery. The cannonade had been relentless, a hammer to the city's anvil; its removal was not for points of pride but of survival. Under the cloak of darkness and the shadow of silence, swift and precise actions led to the sabotage of these engines of destruction. This night raid turned the tide and gave the defenders new hope and strength.

Equally pivotal was the deployment of Giovanni da Capistrano, a fiery Franciscan friar whose sermons had whipped the locals—and indeed the whole of Europe—into fervor. Heeding his impassioned calls, thousands of crusading volunteers converged upon the besieged city. Like a divine clarion, his ardent faith pierced through the despair, galvanizing men to feats of heroism they might have thought inconceivable. This convergence marked a dramatic shift, for it united a fractured populace against a common foe.

An extraordinary moment of valor arose when Hunyadi's troops employed a pontoon bridge to cross the Danube River. This maneuver, fraught with peril, showcased the ingenuity and resilience of their leadership. As they secured this critical passageway, it became evident that the forces of Christendom were determined to leave no stone unturned in their quest for victory. Such was their tenacity that it invigorated all and sundry who witnessed their unflagging spirit.

A poignant scene unfolded before the gates where the Grand Vizier's elite Janissaries clashed with Hunyadi's seasoned veterans. Here, the grim dance of warfare bore witness to instances of sheer heroism and catastrophic defeat. Hunyadi's keen understanding of Ottoman tactics allowed him to anticipate and counter many of their moves, leading to a series of skirmishes that steadily eroded the invading army's morale. Each engagement, an intricate chess move leading ever closer to the longed-for checkmate.

The arrival of July 22nd heralded yet another critical juncture. As the sun rose, so did the spirits of the defenders. Inspired by the visible weakening of their adversaries, Hunyadi led his forces in a comprehensive assault that sought to capitalize on the previous day's successes. This enigmatic push was a blend of brute force and tactical genius, culminating in a confrontation that saw both sides teetering on the precipice of total collapse. The echoes of trumpets, the clangor of steel, the war cries—they all resonated with the urgency of the do-or-die moment.

But the battle was not merely about physical might; it was a testament to psychological warfare. A critical turning point came when the Ottomans, sensing a crack in their psyche, attempted to regroup. Hunyadi, ever the astute commander, seized this moment of hesitation. He ordered a feigned retreat, luring the Ottomans into a trap that sprung with lethal precision. This cunning ruse decimated the Sultan's forces, leaving them scattered and disoriented, while the defenders surged with renewed vigor.

Hunyadi's mastery over the battlefield was complemented by the indomitable spirit of his men. A lesser-known but equally momentous moment was when a contingent of defenders, deemed too inexperienced for frontline combat, conducted a surprise attack from within the city walls. This unexpected sortie breached enemy lines, capturing crucial supplies and boosting morale. Such acts of unexpected courage not only punctuated their defense but also eroded the enemy's fighting spirit.

The Sultan himself, Mehmed II, recognized these turning points and the cascading effect they had on his aspirations. Each setback experienced by the Ottomans was met not just with loss of men and material but a decline in morale that even the most formidable of sieges could not overcome.

His plans, grand and sweeping, began to unravel in the face of Hunyadi's defensive ingenuity and the psychological tenacity of his men.

As the battle reached its zenith, a dramatic turn occurred with the supposed celestial intervention. Reports of an angelic figure appearing before the charge of Capistrano's crusaders spread like wildfire. Whether anchored in divine truth or human fabrication, this apparition spurred on the soldiers as if Providence itself wove into the very fabric of their fighting sinews. The supernatural, mingling with the mortal, brought forth a resurgence among the crusaders, compelling them towards victory.

The climatic collapse of Ottoman resolve cannot be understated. In the decisive hours, the besieged transformed into besiegers. Hunyadi, along with his steadfast comrade Capistrano, led a final, thunderous charge that breached the Ottoman camp. Pandemonium reigned amid the Sultan's forces, a chaotic downfall illustrating that battles are not merely won by blades but also by the mettle and resolve of spirit. The ground trembled under the combined roars of triumph and screams of retreat, an ephemeral mix of agony and exultation.

These key moments and turning points indubitably solidified the Battle of Belgrade as a pivotal event in the annals of Christendom. This was not just the heroism of a single man or his troops but the resilience of a unified front, emboldened by faith and strategic brilliance. The significance of these critical junctures extends far beyond the battlefield, resonating through the centuries as a testament to the power of divine providence entwined with human endeavor. As the word spread of Hunyadi's victory, it echoed throughout Europe, galvanizing future generations to stand against the tides of conquest.

Thus, the Battle of Belgrade remains etched in history, not merely as an episode of martial prowess but as a saga rich with moments of valiant resolve and divine uncertainty. Each moment and turn, each decision and counter, pivoted the fate of nations and faith, shaping a legacy that would endure across the ages, inscribed eternally in the annals of time. From these reverberating skirmishes and salient victories emerged a narrative that was as much about human tenacity as it was about divine intervention, forever engraved in the chronicles of Christendom's triumphs.

Chapter 7: Divine Intervention in Battle

On the hallowed fields of Belgrade, where steel clashed and blood seeped into the sacred earth, there occurred a spectacle that transcended the mortal realm. Reports from the valorous soldiers recount celestial apparitions and inexplicable phenomena that swayed the tide of battle. As the blessed sun hung low, casting fervent rays upon the embattled Christian legions, an ethereal vision of Saint John the Baptist appeared, rallying the weary and invigorating their resolve. The air thickened with a divine presence; angelic hosts were seen descending upon the enemy ranks, shielding Hunyadi's warriors with a celestial aegis. This miraculous intervention, as chronicled by numerous witnesses, was swiftly interpreted as a sign of divine favor. It conferred not only protection but fortitude, guiding them to a victory sanctified by Heaven itself. Such sublime intercessions, in the eyes of many, rendered the triumph of Belgrade not merely a military conquest, but a manifestation of divine will, resonating deeply within the annals of Christendom.

Eyewitness Accounts of Miraculous Events

Thus, as the battle raged fierce and unrelenting, the chronicles of those present bore witness to a spectacle of events most miraculous, evoking divine marvels that none could deny. Amidst the clash of swords and thunderous roars of cannonade, observers chronicled a series of inexplicable phenomena that seemed to proclaim the intervention of the Almighty.

Father Giovanni da Capistrano, a Franciscan friar of unyielding faith, was an eyewitness to the divine interventions that seemed to guide Christian forces to triumph. As he lifted his eyes to the heavens, he recounted seeing a celestial apparition. A figure, ostensibly Saint John the Baptist, holding a gleaming sword aloft, radiated a light so resplendent, it lit the darkened skies. This divine vision rallied the beleaguered troops, fortifying their hearts with renewed courage and fervor.

Father Capistrano's visions were not fleeting wisps borne of desperation. Others too, including soldiers and townsfolk, reported glimpses of angelic hosts descending upon the battlefield. These ethereal beings, bearing the standard of the cross, appeared to fight alongside the weary warriors. Their spectral presence seemingly dulled the enemy's blades and turned back the Ottoman onslaught with a force beyond human ken.

The accounts gathered from the common soldiers and citizens of Belgrade tell of the utter confusion within the ranks of the Ottoman army. It was widely spoken that the advancing Turks, formidable and numerous, were seized by a sudden and inexplicable terror. It was as though an unseen hand had sown chaos and fear in their hearts. Records describe how entire divisions faltered, turning away from the fray, inexplicably retreating as if pursued by some unseen force.

Pious women of Belgrade, gathered in fervent prayer, were also said to have witnessed signs of divine import. Indeed, the town's devout reported a luminous cross appearing in the sky, shimmering with an otherworldly glow. This celestial beacon hung above the fortress, as if serving as a divine shield protecting the stronghold and its defenders.

On that fateful day, the miraculous wasn't limited to the battlefield alone. The waters of the Danube, so often a natural barrier and tactical concern, behaved in unusual ways. Several accounts claim that the mighty river, stirred by unfathomable currents, impeded the movements of the Ottoman fleet. Their vessels were driven aground or turned adrift, rendering their naval maneuvers impotent against the waves that now seemed an instrument of divine will.

A sergeant by the name of Benedek, a soul of humble beginnings and simple faith, swore under solemn oath that he witnessed the Holy Mother herself descending upon the ramparts. Brighter than the morning sun, her visage banished despair and replaced it with hope. Benedek and his fellow soldiers, emboldened by the sacred sight, fought with a vigor and tenacity that defied mortal limits.

Nor were these vignettes of faith confined solely to the embattled city. Across Europe, in cathedrals and chapels, the faithful reported visions that mirrored those seen at Belgrade. The pope's decree to ring the noon bells in unison became not just a call to prayer, but a cry heard even in the spiritual realms. It was claimed that the resonance of these bells carried divine energies, enwrapping the Christian soldiers in a protective embrace.

Legend has it that even Sultan Mehmed II himself reportedly experienced disturbing dreams and waking visions. It is whispered that the conqueror of Constantinople saw a vast, radiant figure towering over his tent, eyes burning with righteous wrath. This spectral judge pronounced doom upon the transgressor, striking such dread in the heart of the sultan that it is said to have shaken his resolve.

The chronicles further recount a moment when, in the thick of combat, a swarm of locusts, inexplicably emerging at an unusual time of year, descended upon the Ottoman encampments. These creatures, harassing and confounding the invaders, left the Christians unharmed, their fields and stores untouched by the pestilential cloud.

Also, the famed military genius John Hunyadi himself bore witness to the miraculous on multiple occasions. Known for his unerring strategies and steely composure, even Hunyadi was brought to his knees, giving thanks to divine providence. He spoke of angelic messengers who, in moments of dire need, revealed to him key tactical maneuvers, saving his men from seeming inevitable defeat and death at the hands of the enemy.

In yet another astounding testimony, an aged monk from the local monastery, a man known for his solitary and meditative disposition, proclaimed that he communed directly with Saint Michael. The Archangel, protector of all Christians, allegedly whispered celestial counsel, which was passed on to Hunyadi. Some believe it was these divine stratagems that turned the tide of the battle at its most critical junctures.

- Angelic apparitions in the sky
- Saint John the Baptist wielding a radiant sword
- Swarms of locusts thwarting the Ottoman army
- Sudden shifts in Danube's currents hampering Ottoman naval forces
- Visions of the Holy Mother descending on the ramparts
- Noon bells as a conduit of divine energy

Even the city's own fabric seemed imbued with righteousness. The very stones of Belgrade's walls, ancient and resolute, appeared to exude an incorruptible spirit. Some soldiers claimed that mortal wounds healed as if touched by the hands of saints, and arrows that struck home were found oftentimes lodged in armor, mere inches from fatal organs.

Finally, there was the inexplicable unity and endurance among the population. The defenders, a medley of soldiers, peasants, and religious, showcased a resilience that by all accounts defied human limits. The varied testimonies spoke of an omnipresent grace, bestowing strength, resolve, and a surpassing will to persevere. It was as if each heart beat with the fervor and purpose of a thousand souls, unified in divine purpose.

While historians may debate the veracity of each of these events, dismissing them as mere coincidences or products of fervid imaginations, the fact remains that the Battle of Belgrade was showered in acts of wondrous nature. And so, posterity remains enraptured by these accounts, seeing in them not merely stories of old but testament to the unshakable faith that carried John Hunyadi and his valiant legions to a victory that echoed through the annals of time.

Theological Interpretations of the Victory

To mull over the events that unfolded at the Battle of Belgrade is to wander through a labyrinth of divine mystery and martial valor. The clash, an orchestra of swords and faith, heralded not just a military triumph but a celestial affirmation. Pious leaders and learned theologians sought meaning beyond the mundane, probing the heavens for traces of divine grace that had descended upon the field of conflict.

First and foremost, one cannot ignore the deep-seated belief among contemporaries that the victory was divinely orchestrated. The Christian forces, led by John Hunyadi, were vastly outnumbered by the well-oiled war machine of the Ottoman Empire. Yet, against these insurmountable odds, the Christian soldiers prevailed. It was as though an invisible hand guided their swords, shielded their bodies, and bolstered their spirits. This perception was not mere superstition but a deeply ingrained theological lens through which the people of the time viewed their world.

Consider the celestial signs that were reported. Many chroniclers noted strange atmospheric phenomena: glowing lights in the sky and peculiar weather conditions that seemed to favor the Christian troops. To the medieval mind, such occurrences were not dismissed as mere coincidence; they were divine omens. These signs were viewed as manifestations of God's will, annunciations that the battle was favored by the Almighty.

The juxtaposition of Hunyadi's astuteness and divine intervention forms the heart of this narrative. The Blessed Mother herself was said to have interceded on behalf of the beleaguered Christians. Visions and apparitions of Mary were reportedly seen by soldiers on the battlefield. It was believed that she guided their hands, their strikes imbued with heavenly strength. For many, this celestial endorsement bestowed upon Hunyadi's triumph a sacred legitimacy, ensuring that his victory would be etched into the annals of Christian lore.

The theological interpretations extended beyond mere celestial imagery. The intrepid soldiers of Christendom, standing steadfast under the banner of the cross, were believed to be modern-day Crusaders, appointed by divine will to guard Europe from the encroaching Ottoman wave. In their triumph, theologians saw echoes of biblical battles where small, righteous forces overcame greater, godless foes by God's command. The tale of David and Goliath springs to mind, a tale revered in both sacred scripture and the hearts of the faithful.

Within the cloisters and study halls of the Church, monks and scholars debated the deeper meanings of the victory. Theological treatises were penned, dissecting the divine elements of the conflict. Many posited that the victory was a test of faith and resilience, a heavenly trial that the Christians had splendidly passed. Others argued that the battle represented a pivotal moment in a cosmic struggle between good and evil, with the forces of light pushing back against the shadow of tyranny and oppression.

It's also crucial to remember the role of prayer and penance before the battle. Pope Callixtus III had previously decreed that church bells should ring at noon each day, calling all Christians to prayer for the success of the Crusaders. This decree was not merely a call for solidarity but a theological act, a collective invocation for divine favor. The ringing bells and joined prayers intertwined the earthly with the divine, making the eventual victory a manifestation of those impassioned supplications. When the news of the Christian triumph spread throughout Europe, these prayers were seen as answered, an undeniable testament to God's active participation in the world.

The presence of relics and sacred artifacts on the battlefield further cemented the notion of divine intervention. Holy relics were carried into battle, believed to carry the blessings of saints and martyrs. The banner of Christendom, adorned with these relics, was seen as a beacon of divine favor. When the winds of battle blew in favor of the Christian soldiers, it was seen as the immemorial power of these sacred objects coming into play, shielding and guiding the warriors.

Yet, the divine endorsement also meant a stern obligation for those who remained. The Church preached that such a victory was to be a beacon of Christian unity and devotion. The theologians interpreted the victory as a divine reminder of the responsibilities that divine favor entailed. Europe was to remain steadfast in its faith, its leaders righteous, and its people devout. Anything less would be seen as an insult to the divine grace that had been bestowed upon them.

In examining the contemporaneous accounts and subsequent theological musings, the insistence on divine intervention is not merely the tale of a miraculous battle but also a story of communal faith and divine intimacy. Belgrade, thus, became not just a site of military success but a sacred ground, consecrated by the Almighty's favor. This perception created a lasting legacy, a spiritual victory that stood both as a divine gift and a solemn charge for Christendom.

Indeed, the victory at Belgrade was more than a historical event. It became a theological emblem, a divine token that resonated through cathedrals, monasteries, and the hearts of the faithful across Europe. It reaffirmed the belief in a providential God, actively shaping the destiny of nations and guiding His chosen people to triumph over adversity. The theological interpretations of the victory thus serve not just to explain an extraordinary event in human terms but to elevate it into the realm of the sacred, a celestial narrative of hope, faith, and divine benevolence.

Chapter 8: The Noon Bells and European Unity

The clanging of the noon bells, decreed by Pope Callixtus III, transcended the mere tolling of metal, resonating instead as a symbol of European unity and resistance. Across the diverse landscapes of Christendom, from the Gothic cathedrals of France to the humble chapels of Hungary, the bells became a clarion call for solidarity against the encroaching Ottoman menace. This decree, an intertwining of faith and defiance, fortified a sense of collective identity among varied European peoples. As each bell rang, it was as though the spirits of warriors and common folk alike were summoned to a shared purpose. The reverberations echoed not only through valleys and villages but through the very hearts of those who had faltered, invigorating their resolve and signaling an unbreakable communal bond. Thus, the ringing of the noon bells did more than commemorate victories; it welded together the disparate factions of Europe, drawing them into a united front that would not so easily be shattered by external threats. This orchestrated harmony, a testimony to the power of coordinated faith, heralded a newfound era of interdependence and mutual vigilance, marking a chapter in history where the shared chime of bells lit the way to unity and resilience.

Implementation of the Decree Across Europe

After the resounding triumph of John Hunyadi at the hallowed Battle of Belgrade, Pope Callixtus III decreed that church bells toll at noon to commemorate the victory and call the faithful to prayer. This proclamation, acting as an authoritative echo across the vast dominions of Christendom, intertwined the sacred with the temporal, binding Europe's diverse lands in a symphonious celebration of piety and unity.

The pope's decree emanated from the heart of the Church, unfurling like a banner across dioceses and parishes. Local bishops and priests became its heralds, their voices resonating through cathedrals, chapels, and village churches. The immediate acceptance of this decree underscores not just the papal authority but a collective willingness to embrace shared rituals in the aftermath of a divine intervention perceived at Belgrade.

In England, where the realms of the monarchy and the Church entwined intricately, the noon bells' implementation was both prompt and poignant. The majestic Ludlow and Canterbury cathedrals, along with rustic parish churches, began to see the sun at its zenith as a moment sanctified by sound. Here, radical yet hallowed incantations and ceremonies adapted to include this ethereal melody. This resonated deeply, acknowledging the European unity stoked by Hunyadi's victory.

Germany, with its confederation of principalities and duchies, revealed a tapestry of responses. Each principality, bound by its unique customs, uniformly adopted the noon bells, yet added distinct flavors to the pious ritual. The imperial cities, such as Nuremberg and Mainz, with their towering steeples, took pride in magnifying the decree with grand processions. These processions merged pageantry and prayer, weaving a communal conscience strengthened by the shared resonance of the midday bells.

Moving to the vast plains and rolling hills of France, the vibrancy of the decree's implementation found a habitat not only in bustling cities but also in tranquil hamlets. Saint-Sulpice and Notre Dame embellished the decree with elements of French religiosity and artistic expression. The Parisians embraced noon bells as a call to remembrance and repentance, marking a divine interval within their splendid tapestry of daily life. The bells reverberated through markets and along the Seine, touching the humble and elite alike.

Italy, the proud cornerstone of Christendom, where papal influence held profound sway, saw a unified and fervent observance. Cities such as Florence, Venice, and Milan adopted the noon bells with great enthusiasm. Here, the decree interwove with liturgical splendor and the artistic soul of the Renaissance. The harmonious peals accompanied the bustling artisans and contemplative monks alike, their sounds shaping a divine cadence within the day's rhythm.

In Spain, still characterized by its reconquista spirit, the noon bells unified regions divided by Moorish and Christian rule. Grand cities like Seville, Toledo, and Barcelona saw the decree as a reinforcement of Christian identity and solidarity. Here, the noon bells transcended their liturgical function, becoming symbols of defiant faith and burgeoning unity amidst cultural confluence.

Thus, in Portugal, the noon bells resonated not only through the mainland but also across its expanding maritime empire. Lisbon's grandeur and the simplicity of coastal chapels echoed the noon bells, inseparably linking maritime ventures with divine protection. Mariners, setting forth on uncharted seas, took solace in the midday peal, imagining their homeland's prayers charting their course.

While Scandinavia lay on the fringes of the papal world, the decree still reached its shores, though tempered by rugged landscapes and sparse settlements. In Sweden, Denmark, and Norway, the noon bells gained meaning not just as religious reminders but as embodiments of a faith stitching distant lands to the core of Christendom. The harsh winters and isolated fjords seemed gentler within the unity tolled by the midday bells.

In Eastern Europe, the decree met a landscape steeped in Orthodox traditions. Yet, even here, the noon bells found resonance. In Poland, Hungary, and the Baltic states, where the Catholic Church exerted growing influence, the decree signaled a harmonious blend of Roman rituals and local pieties. The diverse locales embraced the noon bells as an emblem of resistance against Ottoman encroachment and as a call to cherished unity under Christ.

This resounding embrace across Europe illustrates not just compliance but a shared spiritual and social identity. The decree's implementation evolved beyond a mere mandate, becoming a living testament to Hunyadi's legacy and the broader tale of communal unity fashioned in the crucible of conflict.

Thus, it was that the noon bells would ring out across the realms, suggesting not just the passing of hours but the steadfastness of faith and the collective strength of Europe. The shared observance fostered an indelible bond, each tolling sound a reminder of shared victory, faith, and a potent symbol of unity that would echo through the corridors of history, well beyond the immediate aftermath of the Battle of Belgrade.

While scholars and clergy might differ on the decree's theological implications or its comprehensive impact on societal practices, it is irrefutable that it stitched the many tapestries of European lands into a grandiose, unified patchwork. The noon bells, therefore, stand as an enduring relic, one that hearkens back to a pivotal moment when Europe, in all its diversity, found solace and strength in unity, orchestrating their lives to a singular, sacred rhythm.

Impact on European Societal Cohesion

The resounding peal of the noon bells, initiated by Pope Callixtus III, reverberated not only through the bustling towns and serene villages of Christendom but also through the social fabric of Europe itself. Their melodic chimes called believers to remember the valiant struggle at the Battle of Belgrade, a victory attributed to divine intervention and the martial prowess of John Hunyadi. But beyond mere remembrance, these bells molded the identity and unity of a continent facing the gravest of threats.

In an age fraught with political fragmentation and regional rivalries, the ringing of these bells every midday provided a rare moment of collective reflection for the children of Christendom. The shared ritual of pausing at noon served to weave a cohesive tapestry among disparate peoples. At that moment, every soul under the cross was reminded not only of the victory at Belgrade but of their shared faith, their common enemy, and the divine favor that still rested upon them.

The very act of synchronized reverence, spreading from the Iberian Peninsula to the steppes of Russia, imbued the populace with a sense of belonging to a greater whole. The significance of this cannot be overstated. Europe, at the time, was a patchwork of feuding kingdoms and principalities, each with its own unique customs, dialects, and rivalries. Yet, the noon bells broke through these divisions, creating a daily moment of unity, fostering a sense of collective identity.

The noon bells also served as a clarion call to the chivalric ideals and Christian virtues exemplified by Hunyadi himself. Each peal was a reminder of the virtues of bravery, faith, and sacrifice. For the knights and nobles, the bells recalled the chivalric duty to protect Christendom. For the common folk, they symbolized divine protection and the power of collective prayer. This common memory and shared call to action strengthened the social bonds within and between communities.

Furthermore, the ringing of the bells had a democratizing effect. The sound carried over city walls and rural hamlets alike, touching both noble and peasant. It did not discriminate by rank or station; all were united in their moment of prayer. This daily practice of unity contributed to a nascent sense of equality under the eyes of God, a precursor to the more explicit democratic ideals that would emerge in later centuries.

In monasteries and universities, scholars and monks contemplated the theological implications of the Battle of Belgrade. The noon bells became a subject of scholarly discourse, appearing in sermons, treatises, and philosophical debates. This intellectual engagement strengthened the intellectual cohesion of Europe, as ideas and texts circulated widely, transcending regional boundaries and fostering a shared intellectual culture.

In the cultural sphere, the noon bells inspired art, music, and literature. Poets and composers drew upon the imagery of the bells to evoke the unity and resilience of Europe. Paintings and sculptures depicting the battle and its aftermath became fixtures in churches and public spaces, serving as visual reminders of the collective struggle and divine favor. These cultural artifacts further solidified the collective memory and shared identity forged through the daily ringing of the bells.

The noon bells also served as a form of psychological fortification against the omnipresent threat of Ottoman expansion. Every midday chime was a reminder that the victory at Belgrade was not just a historical event but an ongoing testament to the resilience and divine favor granted to Christendom. This psychological reinforcement was crucial in maintaining morale and unity during subsequent conflicts with the Ottomans.

The symbolic power of the noon bells was also reflected in the diplomacy and alliances of the time. European rulers, despite their rivalries, found common ground in the face of the Ottoman threat. The shared ritual of the noon bells served as a reminder of their collective responsibility to defend Christendom. This sense of shared purpose facilitated diplomatic efforts and alliances, contributing to a more coordinated and cohesive defense against external threats.

In essence, the noon bells served as a daily reaffirmation of the bonds that held European society together. They reminded all of the virtues of faith and unity in the face of adversity. This shared ritual and the sense of collective identity it fostered played a crucial role in the social cohesion of Europe during a time of great upheaval and uncertainty.
The impact of the noon bells on European societal cohesion is a testament to the power of collective memory and ritual in shaping the identity and unity of a people. Through the simple act of ringing a bell, John Hunyadi's legacy and the divine favor he exemplified lived on, shaping the course of European history and forging a more united Christendom.

Thus, it can be said that the impact of the noon bells on European societal cohesion was profound. They transformed a moment of military triumph into a daily ritual of unity and remembrance, fostering a shared identity amid diversity and division. The noon bells were more than just a call to prayer; they were a call to unity, resilience, and the shared values that defined Christendom. In this way, the legacy of John Hunyadi and the miraculous victory at Belgrade continued to resonate through the daily lives of Europeans, forging a more cohesive and united society.

Chapter 9: Post-Battle Achievements of Hunyadi

After the triumphant clash at Belgrade, John Hunyadi emerged not just as a hero of his people, but as a luminary on the grand stage of Christendom. With valor proven and strategy vindicated, he embarked on an ambitious suite of political and military reforms, fortifying Hungary against future threats and fostering unity among its disparate factions. His sagacious policies fostered a burgeoning sense of nationalism, galvanizing the nobility and common folk alike under a banner of shared purpose. Far beyond the borders of Hungary, Hunyadi's legacy reverberated through the courts of Europe, where his name became synonymous with valor and divine favor. Even in lands as far-flung as the Italian peninsula, his exploits were recounted with a mixture of awe and reverence, cementing his position in the annals of history as both a stalwart defender of the faith and a visionary leader whose impact transcended the immediate and obvious triumphs of the battlefield.

Political and Military Reforms

In the aftermath of the triumphant Battle of Belgrade, John Hunyadi emerged not merely as a victorious commander, but as an architect of profound political and military reforms. The clash with the Ottoman forces had underscored the urgent need for a robust political framework and an efficient military machinery. Hunyadi, with his unparalleled vision and leadership, embarked on a journey to transform the fabric of his realm.

Hunyadi's reforms began with the centralization of political power, an endeavor aimed at unifying the fragmented entities within the Hungarian kingdom. He recognized that a divided nobility could never withstand the might of the Ottoman juggernaut. Through a series of legislative measures, he curtailed the excesses of feudal lords, bolstering the authority of the central government. This consolidation of power enabled swift decision-making and cohesive action, pivotal in times of impending crises.

Moreover, Hunyadi's acumen became evident in his restructuring of the kingdom's administrative framework. He initiated the establishment of regional councils, manned by loyal and capable stewards who ensured the implementation of centralized policies. These councils acted as conduits between the monarchy and the populace, fostering a sense of collective responsibility and civic duty. Under Hunyadi's guidance, the bureaucratic machinery operated with unprecedented efficiency, a testament to his sagacious statesmanship.

The military reforms instituted by Hunyadi were nothing short of revolutionary. A veteran of countless skirmishes and battles, he understood that the traditional feudal levy, with its infrequent convocations and disparate arms, was ill-suited to repel the well-organized Ottoman incursions. To rectify this, he introduced a standing army, a permanent force composed of highly trained soldiers. This standing army, well-equipped and strategically stationed, became the bulwark against external threats.

In an age where the bow and arrow were giving way to more advanced weaponry, Hunyadi was a pioneer. He recognized the transformative potential of firearms and artillery. Consequently, he ensured the procurement and integration of these modern armaments into his forces. This modernization gave his army a technological edge, making them formidable adversaries on the battlefield.

But it was not merely the physical armament that Hunyadi revolutionized; he also overhauled the military hierarchy. Establishing rigorous training regimes, he insisted on discipline and meritocracy within the ranks. Officers were promoted based on prowess and capability, rather than noble birth. This merit-based system nurtured a cadre of elite soldiers and commanders, bound not by lineage but by loyalty and competence.

Equally visionary were Hunyadi's foresights into the importance of intelligence and reconnaissance. He organized an extensive network of scouts and informants, whose sole duty was to gather and relay information about enemy movements, strengths, and weaknesses. This intelligence apparatus allowed for preemptive actions and ambushes, often catching enemies unawares and leading to decisive victories.

On the political front, Hunyadi was a master of diplomacy. Understanding that military might alone was insufficient, he sought alliances with other European powers. His diplomatic efforts extended beyond Hungary, weaving a complex web of treaties and agreements with neighboring states and principalities. By fostering these alliances, he ensured that Hungary was not isolated in its struggle against the Ottomans.

One of the most significant political reforms was the establishment of the Diet of Hungary as a legislative body with real power. By involving the nobility and ecclesiastical figures in decision-making processes, Hunyadi created a sense of shared governance. This inclusivity mitigated internal strife and engendered a unified front against external aggressors.

Furthermore, Hunyadi's reformative zeal extended into the realm of justice. Instituting legal reforms, he aimed to establish a more equitable system of law. His courts were famed for their impartiality, and justice was meted out without regard for social standing. These legal reforms engendered a sense of fairness and order, crucial for the stability and prosperity of the kingdom.

The economic reforms accompanying his political and military strategies were crafted to support a sustainable war effort. Recognizing the need for a stable revenue stream, Hunyadi restructured the kingdom's taxation system. Establishing a more efficient tax collection mechanism, he ensured that funds were timely and adequately directed towards military expenditures. Furthermore, he encouraged trade and commerce, understanding that a prosperous economy was essential for a resilient state.

In the arena of agriculture, Hunyadi incentivized the cultivation of lands that had long lain fallow. By offering protection and benefits to those who tilled these lands, he increased the kingdom's agricultural output. This surge in productivity not only fed the populace but also sustained the army, ensuring that the forces remained robust and well-provisioned.

Social reforms were also a part of Hunyadi's vision. He was keenly aware of the power of propaganda and morale. Instituting measures aimed at fostering national pride, he encouraged the documentation and dissemination of Hungary's military triumphs. Poets and chroniclers were commissioned to eulogize the valor of Hungarian warriors, creating a cultural milieu that celebrated heroism and sacrifice.

Underpinning all these reforms was Hunyadi's deep-rooted faith. His decisions were often imbued with a sense of divine purpose. He was a fervent advocate for Christianity, viewing the struggle against the Ottomans as a holy war. This religious zeal permeated his policies, influencing not only the governance of the realm but also the spirit of his people.

In conclusion, John Hunyadi's reforms in the political and military spheres were intricate tapestries, meticulously woven to create a resilient and formidable nation. His visionary leadership, marked by a blend of pragmatism and idealism, transformed Hungary into a bastion of strength and stability. The echoes of his reforms resonated far beyond his lifetime, leaving an indelible imprint on the annals of history. Through the annals and chronicles, his legacy as a reformer and a guardian remains immortalized, a testament to his unparalleled contributions and unwavering dedication to the cause.

Hunyadi's Legacy in Hungary and Beyond

In the aftermath of the valorous Battle of Belgrade, John Hunyadi's legacy unfurled like the dawn of a new era, not only in Hungary but across the vast expanse of European Christendom. His name, indelibly etched in the annals of history, became synonymous with indomitable courage, astute leadership, and unparalleled devotion to the cause of Christian unity.

Within Hungary, Hunyadi's triumph heralded a period of both political and military rejuvenation. The nation, once beleaguered by continuous Ottoman threats, found in Hunyadi a beacon of hope and resilience. His battlefield accomplishments transcended mere tactical brilliance; they embodied a strategic vision for Hungary's stability and security. Following the victorious skirmishes, he undertook numerous reforms to fortify the nation's defenses, ensuring that Hungary would stand as a bulwark against future incursions.

An illustrious aspect of Hunyadi's legacy lay in his adept reshaping of military paradigms. He meticulously reorganized the Hungarian army, incorporating lessons harvested from the conflict at Belgrade. His introduction of more structured training regimens and advancements in siege warfare tactics ensured that Hungarian forces were better prepared for subsequent confrontations. These reforms, seminal in their impact, secured Hungary's military prowess for generations to come.

Equally consequential were Hunyadi's political contributions. As a statesman, he championed policies that strengthened the administrative apparatus of Hungary. His political acumen fostered a more cohesive national identity, uniting various noble factions under a central authority geared towards the common cause of defending Christendom. This consolidation of power was instrumental in establishing a more resilient and unified state apparatus.

Beyond the borders of Hungary, Hunyadi's legacy radiated a profound and far-reaching influence. Notably, his triumph at Belgrade invigorated the morale of European nations, infusing them with renewed zeal to resist

Ottoman encroachments. His success served as a catalytic event, galvanizing a spirit of unity among the disparate sovereignties of Europe. The resounding victory underscored the power of collective action, reminding the continent of the potency inherent in a united Christian front.

Hunyadi's legacy also enriched the cultural and intellectual fabric of Europe. His deeds inspired a plethora of literary and artistic endeavors that celebrated his life and accomplishments. Poets, chroniclers, and historians of the era extolled his virtues in their works, ensuring that his memory endured in the cultural consciousness of Europe. This legacy of inspiration perpetuated a spirit of resilience and valor, imbuing contemporary and future generations with the ideals epitomized by Hunyadi.

The influence of Hunyadi's legacy transcended military and political domains, permeating theological contemplations across Christendom. The miraculous nature of the victory at Belgrade was often perceived as divine validation of Hunyadi's mission. Clerical scholars and theologians expounded upon the battle's spiritual dimensions, interpreting Hunyadi's triumph as a manifestation of divine favor. This narrative fortified the spiritual resolve of the European populace, intertwining Hunyadi's legacy with the sacred mission of defending the faith.

In the broader context of European history, Hunyadi's victories and subsequent reforms acted as a bulwark against the expansionist ambitions of the Ottoman Empire. His legacy underscored the crucial role Hungary played in protecting Europe from Ottoman domination. The bulwark established by Hunyadi provided a buffer that afforded Western Europe the time and space necessary to strengthen their own defenses and prepare for future conflicts.

Moreover, Hunyadi's legacy was a precursor to the burgeoning spirit of the Renaissance in Europe. His emphasis on strategic alliances and diplomatic engagements laid a foundation that facilitated cultural exchanges and intellectual collaborations across borders. These interactions fostered a climate conducive to the Renaissance, wherein the intellectual and artistic rebirth of Europe found fertilized ground.

The lasting reverberations of Hunyadi's legacy are felt even in contemporary reflections on European history. His deeds are frequently analyzed in historical discourse, often serving as exemplars of leadership and fortitude. Modern historians and scholars continue to mine the rich vein of Hunyadi's contributions, uncovering insights that illuminate the epochal significance of his life and achievements.

Summarily, John Hunyadi's legacy is a tapestry woven with threads of valor, strategic genius, and unwavering faith. His contributions not only fortified Hungary but also fortified Christian Europe against the burgeoning tide of Ottoman expansion. Through his reforms, leadership, and the indelible mark of his victories, Hunyadi bequeathed a legacy that transcended his era, leaving an indomitable imprint on the pages of history.

Thus, in recounting the post-battle achievements of John Hunyadi, one cannot but marvel at the enduring impact of his legacy, both within Hungary and far beyond its borders. It stands as a testament to the profound and lasting influence one stalwart soul can impart upon the course of history and the collective destiny of nations.

Chapter 10: Long-Term Impact on Christianity

Thus did the resplendent triumph at Belgrade cast a radiant beacon that reached far beyond the immediate triumph of arms. It heralded an epoch wherein the sinews of Christian Europe found renewed vigor, as disparate realms and principalities beheld the potent force of unity against a common foe. The valor displayed by Hunyadi and his compatriots emboldened many a heart, rekindling hope in a beleaguered Christendom beset by the advancing tides of the Ottoman menace. The resonant peals of the noon bells, celebrating divine succor and martial triumph, called forth a symphony of prayer that wove together the spiritual and communal fabric of nations. Thus, in the crucible of combat and the anvil of faith, was forged a long-lasting solidarity amongst the followers of Christ, a testament to the enduring strength birthed through trial and tribulation.

Strengthening of Christian Europe

The embers of the Battle of Belgrade had scarcely cooled when its ramifications began to unfurl across the tapestry of Christendom, weaving a narrative of valor, unity, and divine intervention that emboldened the Christian community. No longer merely isolated kingdoms, the Christian states found themselves galvanized into a formidable coalition, a bastion against the encroaching forces of the Ottoman Empire. The triumph at Belgrade was not simply a military victory; it signaled the dawn of a more cohesive and emboldened Christian Europe.

The fortitude demonstrated by John Hunyadi and his forces did more than repel an invading army; it served as a testament to the potential for unity within Europe's fragmented Christendom. Before this momentous battle, European kingdoms often found themselves at odds, embroiled in internecine conflicts that weakened their defenses against external threats. The sheer scale of the Ottoman threat, however, necessitated a shift in perspective. The victory at Belgrade underscored the notion that unified action was not only possible but essential for the survival of Christendom.

This newfound unity was epitomized by the cooperation between various Christian states. The rallying cry had come from Pope Callixtus III, whose decree for the ringing of church bells at noon called the faithful to persistent prayer. This decree, though a seemingly simple act, solidified the spiritual resolve of Christendom. It emphasized that the battle was not merely against a physical foe but a spiritual adversary as well. The bells that rang across Europe were both a call to arms and a testament to the collective faith of the Christian peoples.

Moreover, the resonance of Hunyadi's victory reverberated through the halls of power, prompting political reforms and strategic alliances. Kings and princes, once consumed by their petty squabbles, began to recognize the necessity of mutual support. The alliances formed in the wake of Belgrade created a network of cooperation that extended beyond mere military aid. There was a growing recognition that Christian Europe had to present a united front, not just in battle but in political and economic endeavors as well.

Thus, the Battle of Belgrade served as a catalyst for political realignment within Christian Europe. Monarchs and nobility, imbued with a renewed sense of purpose, sought to fortify their realms not only against external threats but also against internal discord. Diplomatic efforts were intensified, and the establishment of alliances became paramount. The ethos of unity cultivated by this momentous victory began to permeate through the political and social fabric of Europe.

John Hunyadi himself emerged as a symbol of this newfound strength and unity, his name synonymous with Christian resilience. His leadership and military prowess became a beacon of hope, inspiring not only his contemporaries but also future generations of leaders. The legend of Hunyadi instilled a sense of pride and determination within the Christian populace, reinforcing the belief that the tide could indeed be turned against the Ottoman juggernaut.

The spiritual dimension of the victory, moreover, cannot be overstated. The miraculous elements attributed to the battle reinforced the Christian belief in divine providence. These accounts were disseminated widely, bolstering the faith and morale of the Christian communities. The notion that their prayers had been answered, that divine intervention had played a role in their triumph, served to strengthen their spiritual resolve. This sense of divine favor was instrumental in galvanizing the Christian states, providing not just a political unifying factor, but a deeply rooted spiritual one as well.

Additionally, this strengthening of Christian Europe extended into the socio-cultural domain. The shared sense of victory and divine protection fostered a cultural renaissance that saw the flourishing of arts, literature, and religious thought. The interplay of military triumph and divine grace became a rich vein of inspiration for artists, writers, and theologians, who sought to commemorate and interpret the significance of the Battle of Belgrade within the broader narrative of Christian history.

In the monasteries and courts, scholarly pursuits were energized by the triumph. Intellectuals engaged in chronicling the events, infusing their writings with the dramatic and miraculous elements that characterized the battle. These chronicles found their way into libraries and schools, becoming essential elements of the educational curricula. The stories of Hunyadi's valor and the miraculous occurrences at Belgrade became integral to the cultural identity of Christian Europe, serving as moral and spiritual exemplars for the youth.

The economic implications of this newfound unity cannot be overlooked either. With a more stable and cooperative political environment, trade routes that had been perilous due to infighting and external threats now became more secure. The prosperity that ensued further reinforced the notion that unity was beneficial not only for defense but for wealth and progress as well. Towns and cities, once at the mercy of marauding armies, began to flourish, their markets bustling with activity.

In summation, the Battle of Belgrade marked a pivotal moment in the strengthening of Christian Europe. The victory acted as a catalyst for political, spiritual, and cultural unity, fortifying Christendom against external adversaries and internal conflicts alike. John Hunyadi's legacy, enshrined in the annals of history, became a symbol of the potential for unity and collective action. The resonance of this battle extended far beyond the immediate military triumph, influencing the very fabric of European society and embedding itself into the cultural and spiritual consciousness of the people.

Role of Prayer in Community Unity

In the annals of history, the mighty hand of prayer has frequently proven itself an invisible yet omnipotent force, weaving bonds of unity amidst the sprawling fabric of society. In the medieval epoch, particularly within the tapestry of Christian Europe, communities found in prayer not merely a conduit to the divine, but a scaffold upon which the architecture of unity rested. This notion is particularly salient when examining the enduring legacy of John Hunyadi and the miraculous occurrences surrounding the Battle of Belgrade. Indeed, prayer, in its most sanctified form, served as a glue that bound together the disparate elements of society, creating a cohesive and resilient communal identity that would face and stave off the Ottoman threat.

The collective act of prayer during times of great peril, as epitomized in the tumultuous days leading to and following the Battle of Belgrade, forged an unbreakable bond amongst Christians. Herein lies the profound intertwining of spiritual devotion and communal fortitude. It was through the clarion call instigated by Pope Callixtus III, mandating the noon bells to summon the faithful to prayer, that a sense of shared destiny was cultivated. This decree was more than a mere religious directive; it functioned as a rallying cry that reverberated through cities, villages, and farmlands, forging a unified front in the face of existential threats.

Such a unifying force was not merely symbolic. Prayer wove itself into the everyday lives of the populace, establishing a rhythm of unity and purpose. The act of coming together in shared supplication, whether in grand cathedrals or humble chapels, instilled a collective resilience. Parishioners, regardless of social standing, joined their voices in a symphony of intercession, forming a spiritual bulwark against forces that threatened their very existence.

Equally, the prayers offered in myriad tongues across European Christendom during the tense moments of the Ottoman siege were believed to invoke divine favor. This common practice highlighted the community's recognition of a supernal power guiding their endeavors.

Hunyadi's forces, emboldened by the knowledge that not merely their swords but their prayers wielded power, fought with a fervor that transcended the temporal domain. Their victories were perceived not just as martial triumphs but as spiritual confirmations of divine support.

The efficacy of prayer in unifying communities was further evidenced through the post-battle reverberations. In the aftermath of Belgrade's miraculous defense, the tales of divine intervention, prayed for and received, spread like wildfire across Europe. These accounts didn't just inspire; they galvanized entire regions into a renewed sense of Christian identity and purpose. Prayer meetings and vigils became common practices, where gratitude for deliverance and petitions for continued protection intermingled. This practice fostered a shared historical consciousness, binding together communities with a common narrative of divine favor and collective resilience.

The communal act of prayer also transcended ecclesiastical boundaries, pulling in those who might have been on the peripheries of religious life. During the most trying periods, individuals who rarely darkened the doorstep of a church found solace and solidarity within its walls. The universality of the threat and the shared act of seeking divine intervention brought people together, transcending social, economic, and even national divides. Here, in the pews where neighbor and stranger alike knelt shoulder to shoulder, was formed a unified entity committed to the welfare of Christendom.

Furthermore, the psychological impact of communal prayer can't be underestimated. In times of strife, the collective focus on a singular, higher purpose provided mental fortitude that enabled communities to face trials with unwavering resolve. The shared experience of praying created a collective memory, fostering a sense of belonging and mutual support. When people raised their voices together in prayer, they weren't just communicating with the divine—they were reinforcing their ties to one another and reaffirming their shared values and objectives.

The role of prayer extended beyond immediate wartime unification. Over time, it cultivated a culture of hope and perseverance, enduring long after the sounds of battle had faded. Rituals established during crisis periods became traditions that fortified community ties across generations. Even as new challenges arose, the foundational practice of collective prayer ensured that communities had a spiritual and social anchor, a point of return that reinforced their unity and resilience.

Thus, within the broad narrative of Christianity's long-term impact, prayer stands tall as a beacon of unity. The battle moments that Hunyadi and his compatriots lived through were, in a way, transient, but the spiritual undercurrent of prayer they engendered had a lasting legacy. Each whispered supplication and voiced intercession threaded communities closer, enabling them to face the vicissitudes of time united and resolute. The importance of prayer transcends the battlefield, embedding itself into the cultural and spiritual DNA of Christian communities, ensuring a legacy of unity that echoes through the corridors of history.

In conclusion, the role of prayer in community unity during John Hunyadi's era exemplifies a powerful testament to the enduring strength of collective spirituality. It was through this divine dialogue that communities across Christendom found coherence, courage, and continuity. Prayer not only solicited divine intervention but also served as the communal heart, pulsing with the shared life force of resilience, hope, and unwavering unity. The echoes of these prayers, started during the Battle of Belgrade, have carried on, shaping the spiritual identity of communities for generations, ensuring that the flame of unity kindled in those times of trial continues to burn brightly.

Chapter 11: The Cultural Resurgence

In the wake of John Hunyadi's triumph at the Battle of Belgrade, Europe found itself invigorated with a newfound cultural fervor. This resurgence breathed life into the arts, enriching the very soul of Christendom with masterpieces in painting, sculpture, and literature. The victory not only fortified the bulwarks of Christian Europe against the Ottoman menace but also served as a crucible for a renaissance of intellectual and artistic achievements. The gallant spirit of Hunyadi inspired poets to weave epics, artists to immortalize heroic deeds on canvas, and scholars to delve into the annals of history with renewed vigor. Thus, the reverberations of Hunyadi's valor rippled through the corridors of time, fostering a cultural revival that illuminated the medieval world and prefigured the blooming Renaissance, solidifying his legacy not only as a military savior but also as a beacon of cultural enlightenment.

Artistic and Cultural Contributions

Amidst the tumultuous waves of warfare and the fierce drums of conflict, the legacy of John Hunyadi transcends mere martial victory. Amidst the backdrop of his venerated success at the Battle of Belgrade, we witness a renaissance in art and culture, enriched by the poignant tales of valor and divine intervention that followed his triumph.

Hunyadi's triumph ignited a spark that set alight the hearts and minds of poets, painters, and musicians. It was as if the prevailing winds of victory had blown away the dust of despair, revealing a canvas upon which artists could immortalize the stories of heroism and faith. The once desolate landscapes of Christendom now blossomed with the vibrancy of creative endeavor.

In those years subsequent to the battle, an outpouring of literary works flourished, championing Hunyadi's bravery and God's providence. The parchments bore witness to epic poetry, interwoven with the themes of divine justice and martial grandeur. Scribes chronicled these tales using a flourish of eloquence that captured the imagination of the masses. Churches echoed with hymns and canticles composed to honor this noble knight and the celestial favor that assured his victory.

In the realm of visual arts, monasteries and churches burgeoned with frescoes and altarpieces depicting John Hunyadi. These sacred spaces, adorned with vivid pigments and meticulous craft, became testimonials to his enduring legacy. Artisans, moved by the miraculous events of the battle, painted scenes that radiated both human valor and divine intercession. Hunyadi's image stood resplendent in armor, a symbol of hope and divine preferment, a figure almost saintly in his martial sanctity.

The sculptors too, were not untouched by this wave of inspiration. Statues and reliefs were crafted with an unprecedented fervor, chisel meeting stone in a harmonious dance that gave form to legends. Hunyadi's likeness, oft depicted atop a mighty steed or standing steadfast with sword in hand, came to embody the spirit of resilience and unity against the

Ottoman encroachment. The marble and bronze evoked narratives that ink could not, solidifying his presence in both sacred and civic spaces.

Our gaze must also turn to the musical harmonies that were born from this age, as bards and minstrels serenaded halls and hearths with songs of Hunyadi's deeds. Instruments of every timbre played scores that echoed the beat of courage and the rhythm of faith. The melodies, rich with emotional tenor, enthralled audiences and transported them to the moments of fervent prayer and fierce battle. Hymns dedicated to the sanctified struggle recast church services into exaltations of heavenly favor and martial virtue.

The theatre, too, became a sacred space wherein actors breathed life into the stories of John Hunyadi. Dramatic inquiries unfolded upon the stage, with playwrights weaving narratives that examined themes of divine favor, human frailty, and ultimate triumph. The spectacles captivated the populace, blending historical recitation with moral instruction, thereby ensuring that Hunyadi's tale grappled with the threads of time and memory.

The victory at Belgrade indeed served as fertile soil for the European Renaissance. As scholars and artists across the continent began to absorb the ripple effects of Hunyadi's triumph, there emerged a renewed vigor in pursuit of knowledge and beauty. The climes of Italy, France, and beyond could not remain untouched by the transformative energy radiating from Hungary, now buoyed by a sense of divine mission and military victory.

A burgeoning interest in religious themes within Renaissance art found new inspiration. Paintings and sculptures began to reflect not only the classical ideals but also the contemporary accounts of divine acts and holy wars. Artisans and intellectuals acknowledged the symbiotic relationship between Hunyadi's battles and their creative ventures, subtly referencing these heroic narratives even in works ostensibly unrelated to the conflict.

Indeed, religious iconography experienced a deep infusion of the martial spirit. Icons of saints and martyrs began to bear semblances of warriors, and biblical scenes would oft incorporate allegorical nods to Hunyadi's exploits. Churches and chapels commissioned stained glass windows that did more than reflect light—they cast radiant stories of valor and providence onto the stone floors.

Moreover, the spirit of Hunyadi's crusade extended its influence into the scholastic realms. Universities and newly established centers of learning found themselves invigorated by the cultural resurgence following Belgrade. Scholarly pursuits in theology and history flourished as academics endeavored to contextualize the victory within the broader spectrum of Christendom's eternal struggle against its foes. Manuscripts and treatises were drafted, delving into both the historical significance and theological implications of the victory.

Not solely restricted to the elite, the surge of artistic and cultural production resonated deeply within the broader populace as well. The folk traditions across the region began to incorporate the legendary feats of Hunyadi, embedding these tales within oral histories and communal celebrations. Festive occasions became opportunities to recount and reenact moments from the battle, keeping the memories alive within the hearts and minds of the people.

At fairs and markets, artisans sold intricate woodcuts and illuminated manuscripts depicting scenes from the Battle of Belgrade. These objects of common enchantment served as both art and story, bridging the divine Providence that they believed had aided Hunyadi with the quotidian lives of the viewers. This democratization of art ensured that Hunyadi's legend was not the purview of the scholarly alone but was shared among the masses.

Equestrian tournaments and jousts, though already commonplace, began to reflect the valorization of Hunyadi's martial prowess. Knights partook not merely in sport but as participants within a ritual deeply embedded in the narratives of faith and valor. Pageantry and ceremony reinforced the chivalric values exemplified by Hunyadi, as events were steeped in symbolism, harkening back to the divine favor that had been manifest on the fields of Belgrade.

Thus, the post-victory years, teeming with artistic and cultural efflorescence, presented a multi-faceted legacy. John Hunyadi's military accomplishments and the miraculous battle served as perpetual sources of inspiration, invigorating a cultural renaissance across Europe. This period of rejuvenation nurtured a profound intermingling of faith, art, and communal identity, forever immortalizing Hunyadi in the collective consciousness.

It is here we find the crux of Hunyadi's cultural contribution—not merely in the naked grandeur of victory but in the enduring cascade of artistic fervor and scholarly reflection. His legend, drenched in both divine and martial glory, carved a perennial niche in the pantheon of historical and cultural imagination. As ink flowed and chisels shaped, the echoes of John Hunyadi's deeds resounded through the annals of time, cementing an indelible legacy that continues to inspire and edify the heart of Christendom.

Influence on European Renaissance

The Renaissance, that glorious rebirth of art, culture, and intellect which blossomed in Europe, didst owe much to a variety of factors both grand and subtle. A key, though often overlooked, contributor to this renaissance lay in the valorous exploits and strategic acumen of John Hunyadi. His victory at the Battle of Belgrade in 1456 was not merely a momentous military triumph; it had a ripple effect across the realms of art, culture, and human thought.

Verily, the success of Hunyadi against the formidable Ottoman forces provided a sanctuary, a bulwark for the Christian states of Europe. It halted the Muslim encroachments that threatened not merely territories but the very soul of Christendom. Safeguarding these lands allowed the free flow and flourishing of ideas, unimpeded by the specter of conquest. In these lands, painters, sculptors, philosophers, and scientists felt a renewed vigor to create, unburdened by the dread of impending doom. One might argue that the Renaissance, that effulgent period of human achievement, might have taken an altogether different path had the Ottomans succeeded at Belgrade.

To dwell on specifics, consider the artistic inspirations drawn from that storied conflict. Libraries and halls resonated with tales of divine intervention and human courage. Such narratives spurred an outpouring of creativity. Artisans and painters began to immortalize scenes of the battle, capturing the fervor and faith of the warriors. Their canvases, rich in color and emotion, became a testament to the newfound spirit of resilience and unity that swept Europe.

Aloft among the lilies and laurels, our learned scholars found their inspirations too. They delved into classical texts, rekindling the ancient wisdom lost to centuries of strife and ignorance, and breathed new life into them. These venerable texts, enriched by the contemporary fervor inspired by Hunyadi's deeds, lent themselves to the Renaissance's quest for intellectual rebirth. The scholastic endeavors were not mere academic exercises but fervent pursuits driven by a palpable sense of purpose.

Even the architecture saw transformations influenced by this epoch. Triumph withstood the test of time, erecting edifices that spoke of victory and faith. Churches and cathedrals showcased a symphony of Gothic and Renaissance styles, combining solemnity with aesthetic grandeur. Perhaps, reflect in thou on how structures like St. Peter's Basilica, eventually completed in the Renaissance, epitomized the era's blending of divine inspiration and human ingenuity.

Moreover, the ripples of Hunyadi's victory surged into the realm of literature. Poets and playwrights found a treasure trove of themes to explore. Valor, divine favor, and man's struggle against overwhelming odds became recurring motifs. Bards and minstrels traversed the lands, weaving tales that underscored the sanctity of Christian unity and the Herculean deeds that defended it. History, myth, and legend intertwined, giving rise to epics that glorified this virtuous harmony.

On a more cerebral note, Hunyadi's triumph instilled a sense of optimism, a belief that humanity could indeed triumph over the forces that sought to crush it. This newfound optimism reflected in how European societies began to value human potential, paving the way for humanism's ascent. The idea that humans were capable of great things, that they held within them the divine spark capable of wondrous creativity and thought—this idea found fertile ground in the post-Belgrade Europe. Philosophers such as Desiderius Erasmus and Thomas More wrote of human potential, echoing sentiments that might never have flourished had the continent been shrouded in the pallor of defeat and fear.

In the realms of science and exploration, the air of triumph and curiosity led men to defy the boundaries of the known world. The spirit that had kindled in the fires of Belgrade may well have sparked the voyages of discovery that characterized the Renaissance. Nations, emboldened by unity and safeguarded from immediate threats, turned their gaze outward. Maps were drawn, seas were charted, and new lands discovered in a grand display of human potential and ambition.

Thus, the victory at Belgrade did more than stem the tide of Ottoman conquest; it provided a canvas upon which the Renaissance could paint its masterpieces. It safeguarded the crucible of human thought and creativity from which sprang a veritable deluge of intellectual and artistic achievements. John Hunyadi's legendary feat was both a shield and a beacon, illuminating the path for a Europe on the brink of its cultural and intellectual rebirth.

Behold, as we reflect upon the myriad accomplishments of the Renaissance, it becomes clear that the Battle of Belgrade and the valiant John Hunyadi played a concealed yet pivotal role in setting the stage. While the artisans and thinkers crafted their legacies, the echo of Belgrade's bells, a clarion of unity, urged them onward. Hunyadi's contributions, immortalized in tales of valor, resonate through time as a cornerstone upon which the grand edifice of the Renaissance was built.

Chapter 12: Modern Reflection on Hunyadi's Victory

Through the misty veils of history, one perceives the essence of John Hunyadi's triumph at the Battle of Belgrade, not merely as a distant valorous feat but as an indelible mark upon the tapestry of time. This victory, wrought through a combination of unparalleled martial strategy and purported divine favor, has been scrutinized by scholars and historians alike. In profound reflection, the battle's magnitude stands resplendent, symbolizing the defiance of Christendom against overwhelming odds. Today, the echoes of Hunyadi's gallantry reverberate in the annals of Christian heritage, reminding us of an epoch when faith and fortitude converged on the battlefield. The significance of this clash, though rooted in a time of swords and shields, extends its shadow into contemporary discourse, underscoring the perennial nature of resilience and unity in the face of adversity. Thus, Hunyadi's victory is not merely a relic of the past but a beacon illuminating the enduring struggle for spiritual and temporal sovereignty.

Historical Analysis of the Battle's Importance

In the chronicles of time, the Battle of Belgrade stands as a monumental testament to the valor and strategic prowess of John Hunyadi. A beacon of hope for a fragmented Christendom, the battle witnessed the miraculous intersection of mortal courage and divine favor. To delineate its importance requires a tapestry woven from threads of historical significance, military strategy, and theological interpretation.

The Ottoman Empire, with its inexorable expansion, poised a formidable threat to the Christian realms of Europe. The stakes could not have been higher, as the conquest of Belgrade would have fashioned a gateway for the Sultan's forces into Central Europe—a region rich in resources and ripe for the taking. Thus, Belgrade emerged not merely as a city under siege but as a symbolic citadel of Christian resilience. The very survival of Christendom seemed to hang in the balance.

Hunyadi's victory at Belgrade was not an isolated military triumph; it was the culmination of carefully orchestrated strategies, diplomatic maneuverings, and unprecedented alliances. By uniting disparate factions under a common cause, he created a coalition force that could confront the Ottoman juggernaut. Historians have often marveled at how Hunyadi's reforms revitalized a weary and disorganized European defense mechanism, particularly through innovations in fortification and the use of gunpowder.

From a military perspective, the Battle of Belgrade showcased the efficacy of guerrilla tactics, the strategic use of terrain, and the psychological warfare that unnerved the Ottoman besiegers. Hunyadi's maneuvers confounded seasoned Ottoman commanders, resulting in unexpected and decisive strikes that turned the tide at critical junctures. The application of such tactics not only secured a pivotal victory but also set a precedent that would influence European military doctrines for generations.

Yet, the importance of the Battle of Belgrade transcends the realm of martial exploits. For the faithful, it echoed the providence of divine intervention. The phenomenon of the "Noon Bells," decreed by Pope Callixtus III, reverberated across European towns and villages, amplifying communal prayers for a beleaguered fortress. This collective supplication and its subsequent fulfillment imbued the victory with an aura of sanctity, augmenting its theological significance.

In an age where the separation between the sacred and the secular was almost nonexistent, victories and defeats were interpreted as manifestations of divine will. The timing of the miraculous events—the solar halo witnessed by both Christian and Muslim soldiers and the sudden outbreak of plague in the Ottoman camp—cemented the perception that the heavens had decreed favor upon the defenders of Belgrade. These occurrences are not merely footnotes but critical elements that amplified the battle's historical gravitas.

Furthermore, the resonance of Hunyadi's victory echoed far beyond the immediate aftermath. For the first time in decades, Europe could exhale a collective sigh of relief. The successful defense of Belgrade became a rallying cry that galvanized a fractured continent. It injected newfound vigor into the pursuit of cultural and intellectual endeavors, ultimately sowing seeds for the Renaissance—a period marked by a reinvigorated curiosity and reverence for classical antiquity.

The political landscape of Europe was also indelibly shaped. Hunyadi's feats earned him a venerated status among his contemporaries, cementing his legacy not as a mere warrior, but as a guardian of Christendom. His reforms, both military and administrative, laid the groundwork for subsequent leaders who would continue to hold the line against Ottoman encroachments. The unity fostered by this victory emboldened alliances and fortified the resolve of nations during a time when discord could ill be afforded.

Moreover, the long-term implications for Christianity cannot be understated. The defense of Belgrade acted as a linchpin event that unified an otherwise disjointed European Christendom. The bravery exhibited by Hunyadi and his forces was celebrated in liturgy and folklore, becoming an exemplar of Christian chivalry and piety. The tale of Belgrade was recounted from pulpits to parlors, fostering a collective memory that transcended borders and generations.

In a broader cultural context, the victory at Belgrade inspired a resurgence of artistic and literary production. Poets, painters, and sculptors found in this historic battle ample material to rekindle the fervor of Christian heroism. Works emanating from this inspiration served not merely as commemorations but as cultural artifacts that continued to bolster European identity against the Ottoman 'other.'

Indeed, in assessing the historical analysis of the Battle's importance, one cannot overemphasize its role in altering the trajectory of European history. The symphony of military genius, divine intercession, and cultural renaissance orchestrated by this epic confrontation provided a bulwark against the tides of conquest and subjugation. Hunyadi's legacy endures not merely in annals of history but in the spiritual and cultural fabric of Europe itself.

In sum, the Battle of Belgrade was far more than a clash of arms. It was an epoch-defining episode that preserved the sanctity of Christendom, fostered European unity, and seeded the flowering of the Renaissance. To walk in the shadow of this great historical event is to bear witness to a legacy that continues to inform our understanding of faith, valor, and the indomitable human spirit.

Contemporary Significance and Remembrance

Through the corridors of time, John Hunyadi's victory at the Battle of Belgrade reverberates, far beyond the mist-laden fields where swords clashed and destinies wrought. In the annals of Roman Catholic history and broader European heritage, this triumphald moment has not merely lingered but grown, transforming into a beacon of resilience revered even now. The echoes of this resonant victory affirm the triumph of will, faith, and valor, elements indispensable to our contemporary fabric.

The commemorations of Hunyadi have taken diverse forms, both poignant and grand. In the hallowed halls of scholarly discourse, historians toil to fathom the depths of his strategies and virtues. Each analysis, with its myriad interpretations, serves to renew our understanding of his immense contribution to Christendom's defense. Beyond mere academic indulgence, these discussions foster a widespread recognition of the courage that halted the formidable advance of the Ottoman power, breathing life into legends etched in the collective memory.

Anniversaries of the battle often see the ringing of the noon bells across various locales, a tradition initiated by Pope Callixtus III but sustained by countless generations thereafter. This simple yet profound ritual binds communities in a tapestry of unified remembrance. It is not merely an echo of the past but a vivid reminder of the collective strength and faith that can triumph against seemingly insurmountable odds.

Artistic expressions further cement the remembrance of Hunyadi's achievements. In stained glass, frescoes, and intricate tapestries, artists draw upon the rich palette of his victories. Churches, grand and humble alike, become sanctuaries of his legacy, where faithful gather to draw inspiration from depictions of his heroism. These visual narratives, interwoven with sacred relics, reiterate Hunyadi's steadfastness and divine favor in vivid hues and majestic strokes.

Educational curricula across Europe and parts of the Roman Catholic world, too, ensure that Hunyadi's legacy is instilled within the hearts of the youth. Through reiteration of his strategic brilliance and unwavering commitment to Christendom, young minds are imbued with the significance of his deeds. Textbooks and lectures recount with fervor the resilience of a warrior who, against the throes of overwhelming opposition, emerged as a sentinel of his faith and fortress of his people.

Amid the myriad forms of remembrance, the most potent is the continued invocation of Hunyadi in liturgies and prayers. His name is invoked as a paragon of divine favor and righteous struggle, serving as a spiritual anchor in times of tribulation. This religious and cultural continuity assures that Hunyadi's spirit remains an indelible part of the collective consciousness, enshrining his memory within the sanctum of the faithful's hearts.

However, it is not solely in the religious and educational domains that Hunyadi's legacy thrives. His victories resonate in political echelons too. Leaders and statesmen often draw parallels between contemporary geopolitical challenges and Hunyadi's epoch-defining encounters. His strategic acumen and diplomatic foresight are subjects of acclaim and scrutiny, forming a template of sagacious statecraft and leadership that transcends centuries.

The city of Belgrade itself stands as a living testament to the battle's significance. Monuments and plaques adorn the cityscape, each narrating the valorous saga of Hunyadi and his men. These historical markers are not mere stones but embodiments of a collective reverence that time disciplines to honor perpetually.

In literature, tales of Hunyadi's exploits continue to fuel the imaginations of writers and poets. The dramatic elements of his life, juxtaposed against the grand tapestry of history, provide a fertile ground for epic narratives. These literary endeavors ensure that Hunyadi's sarabande of sword and faith remains intertwined with the cultural consciousness, inspiring generations to reinterpret and rejuvenate his heroic mythos in myriad forms.

Even in modern day Hungary, the heroism of Hunyadi is memorialized through national days of remembrance and state functions. His memory serves as a unifying force, reinvigorating national pride and historical consciousness. As a national hero, Hunyadi's legacy reinforces Hungary's identity and geopolitical relevance in an ever-changing European landscape.

The impact of Hunyadi's victory on contemporary European unity cannot be overstated. The battle demonstrated that disparate Christian factions could coalesce into an indomitable front. This lesson of unity, drawn from the chronicles of Belgrade, continues to inspire modern endeavors toward political and cultural cohesion within Europe. Hunyadi's legacy serves as both a historical reminder and a guiding principle for the continent's collective aspirations and shared values.

In essence, the contemporary significance of Hunyadi's victory at the Battle of Belgrade is a multifaceted tapestry. It weaves together academic discourse, religious reverence, artistic portrayal, educational curricula, political homage, and societal unity into a singular force that perpetuates his memory. Seamlessly integrating the past with the present, the tale of Hunyadi remains an epic yardstick against which courage, faith, and unity are measured and celebrated.

Indeed, John Hunyadi's eternal legacy is a testament to the timeless virtues that define the shared journey of humanity. His victories echo far beyond the annals of history, inscribed in the hearts of all who cherish and uphold the sanctity of faith, the persistence of hope, and the valor of the human spirit. Thus, Hunyadi's legacy shall forever remain an invincible bulwark of inspiration and a cornerstone of enduring remembrance.

Conclusion

As the sun sets on the tale of John Hunyadi and the monumental Battle of Belgrade, we find that the annals of history are forever altered by his deeds. His valor and strategic brilliance not only fortified the Christian bulwark against the Ottoman tide but also ignited a spark of unity and faith across Europe. Through the chiaroscuro of war and peace, devotion and duty, Hunyadi emerges as both a warrior and a guardian of Christendom.

It is of crucial import to remember that Hunyadi's rise was inexorably tied to the broader context of his times. His early life, steeped in militaristic discipline, combined with the harsh lessons of his initial campaigns, sculpted him into the hero we now revere. Yet, it was not mere fortune that fashioned him; his natural acumen for leadership and deep understanding of military stratagem were evident. These qualities bore fruit during the direst hours of his clash with the Ottoman threat.

The medieval epoch into which Hunyadi was born was fraught with peril and opportunity. The ascendancy of the Ottoman Empire was a looming specter over Europe, threatening both territory and treasure. Against this backdrop, John Hunyadi emerged as a bulwark of hope and resilience. His encounters with the Ottomans were not mere footnotes in history, but defining moments in the struggle between cultures, faiths, and empires—a struggle that culminated besidst the ramparts of Belgrade.

Pope Callixtus III, his decrees, and his influence anchored the spiritual undertones of this epochal conflict. The call for unity resounded through the tolling of the Noon Bells, a sonorous reminder of the Church's rallying cry for solidarity and resistance. This papal intervention not only galvanized warriors but also united communities under a common banner of divine providence and Christian fortitude. Thus, Hunyadi's efforts were buoyed by a wave of ecclesiastical support that perpetuated his cause beyond his martial prowess.

As armies prepared for the inevitable clash, Hunyadi's reforms and alliances solidified the ranks of those who stood ready to defend Christendom. His foresight in restructuring military frameworks and securing diplomatic ties set the stage for a formidable defense. These preparations were not merely tactical but bore the weight of a moral imperative to protect and preserve.

In the crucible of battle, Hunyadi's tactical ingenuity came to the forefront. Amidst the din of clashing swords and roaring cannons, key moments were defined by his deft movements and keen grasp of battlefield dynamics. It was not just combat but a theater of strategy and valor, where each turning point carried the heavy promise of either salvation or despair.

The victory of Belgrade was imbued with notions of divine intervention, as chroniclers and theologians alike have attested. Eyewitnesses spoke of miraculous happenings, attributing their triumph not solely to human enterprise but also to divine will. These accounts are woven into the fabric of the battle's legacy, painting a picture of a heavenly realm interceding in earthly affairs.

Furthermore, the effect of Pope Callixtus III's Decree for Noon Bells transcended the battlefield. Its implementation across Europe fostered a sense of unity and purpose, bridging disparate nations under a sacred concord. This cohesion bolstered the societal fabric, imbuing the populace with a steadfast resolve that resonated through the ages.

Post-battle, Hunyadi did not rest on his laurels. His subsequent reforms in both political and military arenas cemented his legacy. His contributions rippled beyond geography to shape the very identity of his homeland, Hungary, and extended their influence far afield. That legacy, intertwined with the annals of European history, remains a testament to his enduring impact.

The triumph at Belgrade strengthened the bulwark of Christianity across Europe. This victory served not just as a military conquest but as a reaffirmation of faith and communal prayer. The collective spirit, bound by a shared trust in divine providence, was invigorated, marking a pivotal moment in the defense of Christian Europe.

In the aftermath of such climactic events, there was a cultural resurgence. The artistry and cultural expressions flourished, feeding into the larger Renaissance that swept through Europe. They bore the indelible marks of a period rejuvenated by the valor and sanctity Hunyadi represented, thus feeding a legacy of enlightenment and creativity.

Modern reflections on Hunyadi's triumph reveal a tapestry rich in historical and contemporary significance. Today, scholars and historians dissect the strategic brilliance and theological reverberations of the Battle of Belgrade, recognizing its profound impact. The remembrance of Hunyadi's heroics serves as a beacon of valor, faith, and unity, reminding us that history is often sculpted by the courage of a few for the salvation of many.

Thus, we conclude our voyage through the life and legacy of John Hunyadi. His story, rife with dramatic battles, divine signs, and lasting reforms, is not merely a chapter in the annals of history. It is a saga of unyielding spirit and indomitable faith. Hunyadi's legacy endures, a beacon that still lights the path for those who view history not just as a recounting of past events, but as a wellspring of inspiration and a testament to human potential intertwined with divine grace.

Appendix A: Primary Sources and Further Readings

In shaping this venerable tome, many ancient manuscripts and venerable writings have served as the cornerstone of our narrative. The triumphs and tribulations of John Hunyadi, and the miraculous saga of the Battle of Belgrade, have been meticulously chronicled through an array of primary sources and scholarly disquisitions. Below, we present an assemblage of these foundational texts and further readings, which weaves the tapestry of Hunyadi's extraordinary life and the epochal events that surround him.

Primary Sources

- **Annals of Janos Thuróczy**: A contemporary chronicle that offers an explicit portrayal of Hunyadi's martial endeavors and the fervor of the Battle of Belgrade.
- **Epistolae et Chartae**: Letters and charters issued by and about Hunyadi, providing firsthand docquets of his diplomatic overtures and military stratagems.
- **The Papal Bulls of Pope Callixtus III**: Encyclicals and edicts that decreed the noon bells, underscoring the ecclesiastical import of the victory at Belgrade.
- **Memoirs of Bonfini**: The historical memoirs penned by Antonio Bonfini, the Italian historian, which elucidate Hunyadi's campaigns and his indomitable spirit.
- **Ottoman Archives**: Documents and correspondences from the Ottoman perspective, shedding light on the multifaceted theatre of this colossal conflict.

Further Readings

1. **The Hunyadi Wars**, by Ivan Boldizsar: A scholarly expedition into the variegated wars led by John Hunyadi and their resonance across

Europe.

2. **Miracles and Martyrdom: The Battle of Belgrade**, by Thomas Fazakas: An interpretive compendium exploring the miraculous occurrences and their theological ramifications.
3. **Papal Power and European Unity**, by Maria Tibor: Detailed analysis on how the decree of noon bells unified Christendom in a symphony of prayer and purpose.
4. **The Siege that Shook Europe: Constantinople and Beyond**, by Stephan Tsaravos: Offers crucial context on the socio-political climate preceding the Ottoman onslaught and Hunyadi's rebuttal.
5. **Hunyadi: The Knight of Light**, by Georg Mezey: A biographical sketch emphasizing the chivalric and humanitarian aspects of Hunyadi's life.

With these texts as our guiding stars, one can journey deeper into the annals of history, grasping the full magnitude of Hunyadi's legacy and the divine intercessions of that fateful battle. May this aggregation of knowledge serve as a beacon to all seekers of truth and valor.